# FINDING YOUR WAY THROUGH GRIEF

## KIM THOMAS

D0096754

HARVEST HOUSE PUBLISHERS

EUGENE, OREGON

Unless otherwise indicated, all Scripture quotations are taken from the New American Standard Bible ®, © 1960, 1962, 1963, 1968, 1971, 1972, 1973, 1975, 1977 by The Lockman Foundation. Used by permission. (www.Lockman.org)

Verses marked NIV are taken from the HOLY BIBLE, NEW INTERNATIONAL VER- SION®. NIV®. Copyright © 1973, 1978, 1984 by the International Bible Society. Used by permission of Zondervan. All rights reserved.

Verses marked NLT are taken from the *Holy Bible,* New Living Translation, copyright ©1996. Used by permission of Tyndale House Publishers, Inc., Wheaton, IL 60189 USA. All rights reserved.

Verses marked NKJV are taken from the New King James Version. Copyright © 1982 by Thomas Nelson, Inc. Used by permission. All rights reserved.

*Cover by Koechel Peterson & Associates, Inc., Minneapolis, Minnesota*

*Cover photo © Photodisc Green/Getty Images*

**FINDING YOUR WAY THROUGH GRIEF**
Copyright © 2004 by Kim Thomas
Published by Harvest House Publishers
Eugene, Oregon 97402
www.harvesthousepublishers.com

Library of Congress Cataloging-in-Publication Data

Thomas, Kim, 1958-
  Finding your way through grief / Kim Thomas.
    p. cm.
  ISBN 0-7369-1033-6 (pbk.)
  1. Consolation.  2. Grief—Religious aspects—Christianity.  3. Thomas, Kim, 1958–
I. Title.
  BV4905.3.T48  2004
  248.8'6—dc22                                                              2004005753

**All rights reserved.** No part of this publication may be reproduced, stored in a retrieval system, or transmitted in any form or by any means—electronic, mechanical, digital, photocopy, recording, or any other—except for brief quotations in printed reviews, without the prior permission of the publisher.

**Printed in the United States of America.**

04  05  06  07  08  09  10  11  / BP-KB /  10  9  8  7  6  5  4  3  2  1

*For those who have said goodbye,*
*and in honor of those who have gone ahead.*

"The Waiting Room" (Kim Thomas, 2003)

# Contents

**The Journey**

1. Rain . . . . . . . . . . . . . . . . . . . . . . . . . . . . . . . . . . . . . 9
2. Grief . . . . . . . . . . . . . . . . . . . . . . . . . . . . . . . . . . . . 13
3. The Anatomy of a Long Goodbye . . . . . . . . . . . . . . . 17
4. The Rehearsal . . . . . . . . . . . . . . . . . . . . . . . . . . . . . 21
5. The News . . . . . . . . . . . . . . . . . . . . . . . . . . . . . . . . . 27
6. The Shadow of Death . . . . . . . . . . . . . . . . . . . . . . . . 31
7. The Dark Night . . . . . . . . . . . . . . . . . . . . . . . . . . . . 37
8. The Goodbye . . . . . . . . . . . . . . . . . . . . . . . . . . . . . . 41
9. The Mourning After . . . . . . . . . . . . . . . . . . . . . . . . . 49

**The Healing**

10. Two Months Later . . . . . . . . . . . . . . . . . . . . . . . . . . 55
11. Faith . . . . . . . . . . . . . . . . . . . . . . . . . . . . . . . . . . . . 59
12. Hope . . . . . . . . . . . . . . . . . . . . . . . . . . . . . . . . . . . . 63
13. Surrender . . . . . . . . . . . . . . . . . . . . . . . . . . . . . . . . 67
14. The Comfort of Friends . . . . . . . . . . . . . . . . . . . . . . 71
15. Higher Purpose . . . . . . . . . . . . . . . . . . . . . . . . . . . . 77
16. Remembering . . . . . . . . . . . . . . . . . . . . . . . . . . . . . . 81
17. Keep Showing Up . . . . . . . . . . . . . . . . . . . . . . . . . . . 87
18. Something Old, Something New . . . . . . . . . . . . . . . . 91
19. Living in the Land of the Living . . . . . . . . . . . . . . . . 95
20. Hankies . . . . . . . . . . . . . . . . . . . . . . . . . . . . . . . . . . 99

**Thirty Days of Meditations**

21. An Invitation . . . . . . . . . . . . . . . . . . . . . . . . . . . . . . 105

Think of yourself just as a seed patiently wintering
in the earth; waiting to come up a flower in the
Gardener's good time, up into the real world, the real
waking. I suppose that our whole present life, looked back
on from there, will seem only a drowsy
half-waking. We are here in the land of dreams.
But cock-crow is coming.

C.S. LEWIS

# The Journey

# 1

# Rain

*When they walk through the Valley of Weeping,*
*it will become a place of refreshing springs,*
*where pools of blessing collect after the rains!*

PSALM 84:6 NLT

It is uncharacteristically gray this Orlando morning. Ironically, I will sit in this chair one week from tomorrow having lost Mom to the brighter lights of heaven, and the sky will be flooded with blue from corner to corner. But not today.

Today the drizzle is overtaken by gentle italic lines of rain. They fall so slowly that I can trace them through the sky to their landing place in the waterway some twenty feet behind the screened-in porch of my parents' house. As I cry long, slow tears, I imagine that heaven has joined in my sorrow and is also weeping long, slow tears. Being the writer in the family, I begin to memorize this moment.

My mom has been sick for a long time. She was first diagnosed on 9/11, the historic day that mothers, fathers, friends, and loved ones were lost to unexpected tragedy. My husband and I spent the morning tightly knotted on our bed in front of the television, fearing that we had lost his mom in the Pentagon explosion. By noon we had received word that she was safe, walking with others to the closest Metro stop in an effort at getting home. Safe. She was out of danger, and we spent our praises.

The phone rang again that afternoon with "Mom" information. This time it was to inform us that my mom had been diagnosed with pulmonary fibrosis. One year and two months later the diagnosis of lung cancer would be added, surreally following a false diagnosis of lung cancer for my father. Today, after a year of her silent suffering, lung surgery, radiation, and a collection of other unbearable symptoms and side effects, Mom was in the hospital with pneumonia and other complications of her disease. She was not safe, or in any way out of danger. I was quietly aware that we were losing her.

Only a week ago, I talked to her on the phone when she gave me the good news. "Honey, it's pneumonia, and they can treat that!" Her hope stretched mine, and I made plans to come and visit her. Two nights later, Thursday, my sister called to say Mom might not make it through the night. That was the two-minute warning God had graciously given us. Today is Sunday, and I am having church in the rain.

As I watch it come through the screened roof on the outer three feet of the porch, I want to feel its gentleness mark a path on my face. So I walk over to the edge and lay on my back, face to the rain, and lose my tears in the weather falling on my skin. God sent me comfort, and my husband lay down beside me in the rain. He silently reached over and held my hand. The intimacy of that morning was pure and unspoken, the stuff of twenty-five years of marriage.

We lay there with the concrete forcing its cold on our skin through delicate layers of pajama and T-shirt. Then the rain stopped without the histrionics of thunder and lightning. In fact, a slight glow dried the sky and my face, and I walked in to shower and get ready to go back to the hospital. In this private little church service, God reminded me with Sunday rain that even Jesus wept.

# 2

# *G*rief

*I thought I could make a map of sorrow.*
*Sorrow, however, turns out to be not a state but a process.*

C.S. LEWIS

The weeping of loss is a long and ever-changing grief. The initial tears bathe away weeks and months of sorrow that have, bit by bit, stolen our hearts. In a long terminal illness, each paragraph of bad news is mourned. And so you lose your loved one a little more each day. After the initial torrent of tears, as the weeks passed after Mom's death, the tears became more sparse for me. I tried to reenter my life and be strong for my dad, who was staying with us those first two months. I was somewhat closed off during that time, only allowing for a few tears to leak out. There was Thanksgiving, Christmas, Dad's birthday, and New Year's. Plenty of distractions to keep us busy, what with decorating, shopping, and cooking. Then when Dad went back home, and I was thoroughly engaged in my writing, moments of exhausting sorrow and tears would fall on me from nowhere. I wept for my own sorrow, for my dad's sorrow, and for the fact that life would never again be the way it was.

It has been a quarter of a year since Mom died. Time has not made everything okay, but it has made it more bearable. I have been through a lot of the "firsts" without Mom: first Christmas, first Sunday in church, first writing, and now I await the first spring, first birthday, first Mother's Day. I have wept at her hospital bed, her memorial service, and her burial. I am ready to remember, and smile.

Death is a most undeniable reality. It is the most obvious scar of the Fall, the most lamentable fact of life. It is the ultimate symbol of separation, our separation from God, and the most palpable experience of that separation. I've never understood the finality of separation better, and I've never longed for heaven more.

Most of my life, I've been afraid of the entire concept of death. My husband, Jim, reminds me that since I have never really made peace with the unfortunate opossums who have become united with the bumper of many a car in this world, how could I possibly make peace with the mortality of humanity, much less that of my beloved ones?

But now I have at least begun to make that peace. That is what this book is about. It is not entirely neat, because death is not. I am not yet in the fluffy clouds or green pastures of comfort about this issue. I am rather in the process of becoming—sure of the hope of heaven yet still frail and vulnerable to my grief. There will be a season for fluffy clouds and lambs, I suppose, but I am not quite there.

I have walked the valley of the shadow of death. It is slow and long. I have peered over the edge from "what has been" into the abyss of "what is yet to be." I have found myself in a puddle of doubt, wondering if perhaps my faith has been all a machination of comfort and niceties, simply a construct of finite minds, and I even find myself wondering if it is true or safe. I have bristled at the clichés of well-meaning people. "They are in a better place now." "You must rejoice if you truly believe in heaven." "You were lucky to have the time with them that you had."

On the other hand, there have been moments of tenderness unlike any before in my life. There have been times of God's presence so real I could feel His breath on my neck. I have found reserves of strength and courage I wasn't aware I could access. I have come to know my dad in ways I never would have before, and I have found that not only is he everything my mother loved, but he is also everything I wanted him to be.

Grief is the collection of emotions resulting from irrefutable change. It is the season in which we come to terms with the notion that things are not the way they are supposed to be. As a person of faith, all of my life I have wondered if in times like these, God would be enough. To my great sigh of relief, I can honestly say He is. Death and the collateral damage ensuing is not how I would choose for things to be, but the sufficiency of a suffering Savior who not only wept over this truth but also experienced death willingly has fortified me. Enough. Still, I am no pillar of unwavering faith. Grief is a process; it changes with each day, emotion, and experience. So I take a deep breath. I am learning to find my way through, and to allow the God of all comfort to carry me when I can't walk, run, or stand.

# 3

# The Anatomy of a Long Goodbye

*We are never ripe until we have been made so by suffering.*

HENRY WARD BEECHER

s long as I can remember, Mom has been my best cheerleader and encourager. She was the first call with good news or bad news. Her response in either case would be the same. "Honey, God is in charge! Aren't we glad?" The sovereignty of God was her repeated song.

A little over a year ago, I entered the frightening territory of beginning to anticipate her loss. She had struggled with various health issues over the years, but they were always things she could cope with and live through. But just after Thanksgiving last year, the diagnosis of cancer entered our world, and it seemed Mom might not be able to power through this problem. Even then, the song was still sung, with an added refrain of "to God be the glory..."

My cousin Cindy is like a sister to me. Eighteen years ago her dad, like a second father to me, died instantly of a brain aneurism five days before his sixtieth birthday. My courageous and sometimes stoic Aunt Gene calmly performed CPR on the love of her life until the emergency medical rescue team appeared and determined he was gone. In an instant, a thriving and vital exclamation of a man was no more. He walked into the closet to put on his shoes, grabbed his head, and said, "Oh, Gene…" and was instantly gone from us.

I remember one of the first things everyone said was "that was how Jess would have wanted to go"—instantly, without a long and lingering illness. And that was true. But I guarantee you he would have chosen for that day to come much later.

This year, after Mom's surgery and then later her radiation treatment, Cindy and I talked about the ways we lose the people we love. She said that she had always felt it was harder to lose someone instantly, the way her dad died, until now. After watching all of us, she decided that a long and lingering illness was far more painful than the sudden sting of her father's passing. I'm not sure there is a way to measure pain or determine which way of loss is harder. I think her empathy for us, and her own pain at watching Mom's progressive decline, was poignant, and that time had probably softened the ache at losing her own dad. What I know is that we don't get to choose how we will say goodbye to the people we love, how they will leave our presence for the brighter lights of heaven. But God gives us little hints and insights as He chooses for our highest good in each situation. As I sat in Nashville on that gray and icy November afternoon, I knew I was about to be acquainted with the anatomy of a long goodbye.

Saying that it is actually a "goodbye" is even a little bit of a stretch. The entire time we didn't really admit we were saying goodbye. It's like watching a movie, and you see someone sick and dying, and you say, "Don't they know she's going to die? Why don't they talk about it?" Well, you don't really talk about it because, if you do, you allow it to be possible. So at first you talk about things like "when you get better," or "when you come home." And then it becomes more like "after you eat some," or "after the medication takes effect," and the entire time what you are doing is just readjusting your hope and making silent peace with the ever-growing reality. You say "I love you" a lot, but you never really say "goodbye."

The important thing is to say whatever needs to be said. To settle what is unsettled. To say, "I'm sorry," or "I appreciate you." To give and forgive. The long goodbye is the opportunity to have no regrets on either side, to serve the beloved one who is dying and the rest of the family who are hurting. For us, it was a time of reshaping our family. It was the preparatory pause, when you do your best to begin to fill the anticipated emptiness with togetherness. And it is a time of reaffirming the most important realities of faith and *Presence*.

# 4

# The Rehearsal

*Sorrows are visitors that come without invitation.*
CHARLES SPURGEON

❧

*I*llness seemed to sneak up on our family like a sudden summer storm. One day we were all planning our lives as though there would be plenty of tomorrows, and the next we had no certainty of any days promised.

Mom had been diagnosed with pulmonary fibrosis on September 11, 2001. That was when my husband began to share with me the truth that "our days do not belong to disease or even doctors, but to our heavenly Father."

We were in the midst of researching various kinds of pulmonary fibrosis, and progressive treatment facilities in the United States in April of 2002. Mom's treatment in Florida seemed to have little urgency and fewer results. The complications of insurance programs, frustration over getting copies of doctor reports and test results, minimal access to physicians for simple questions, and the sheer confusion of all that was happening seemed too much burden for any one of us to carry. So we shared, and each of us took on assignments and tasks.

Mom and Dad bought organizer notebooks and began asking for copies of everything at every appointment. They would come home in the evenings and three-hole punch all the test results and paperwork and file them in the organizers. Dad collected business cards from each office and put them in clear pocket sheets within the notebooks. Those organizers began to symbolize Mom's illness and the process of her dying. So much so that after her death, my sister and I couldn't bring ourselves to go through them or clear them out quite yet.

Just when we had begun to move forward and were about to commit to a new plan of treatment for Mom, Dad had a startling doctor's appointment. The parallels and coincidences were too unreal. Just like Mom, he had been battling an endless cold and bronchitis. He had been to see the doctor and had news to share with us. They called us to set up a conference call between themselves, my sister and her husband, and Jim and me. They set it for 4:00 P.M., two hours later.

The fear of those two hours was the first sting in a long process of fear and coping. Those two hours were a rehearsal for what was ahead. I think one of the things that is so hard to make peace with is that, as with any rehearsing, you begin to get good at what you practice. In this case, you begin to learn how to cool the fire of adrenaline that races through your body, and you shut down any unnecessary emotions so as to conserve your calm. And after the initial encounter with a fatal prognosis, you begin to take the news as if it is a normal part of life. Which it is, but it never was supposed to be.

We huddled by our phones, individuals, but connected by DNA, marriage, tears, memories, and Spirit. Mom and Dad took turns reciting the story. The nurse practitioner in Dad's local doctor's office sat down between him and Mom, held their hands, and told them that the most recent chest X-ray showed that Dad had lung cancer. From bronchitis to cancer in one X-ray.

This was the first time "cancer" became a part of our vocabulary. We would come to be far more familiar with it than we ever wanted to be.

After hanging up the phone, I was ten years old again, lost and confused, unable to speak the words "my dad has cancer." The reality of death—mortality—is something we are not prepared for, ever. We prepare in the sense that it is an unspoken reality, but when it is our reality, everything seems surreal.

That night we went to see a young couple from our church perform with a small comedy improv group in a coffee shop. As I sat at our little table, I looked around the room and thought how nice it would be to be able to simply laugh and enjoy the moment. But didn't they all know that my dad has cancer?

It was almost beyond belief that both Mom and Dad were suffering from extreme lung conditions. So much overlap, yet just the smallest noticeable differences. We were motivated to do research and tie the details together with poisonous air, histoplasmosis, bad water, something. It was like finding a piece for a puzzle that for all visible reasons should fit, but it just doesn't. What looked so obvious seemed to be simply an ironic theme to intimately intertwined lives.

The body is intricate, delicately woven, and rhythmically balanced. We learned how little it takes to disturb such masterful design, and we frailly placed ourselves in God's merciful hand in each moment.

Our concerns now switched from Mom to Dad, feeling that Dad's condition was more acute and life-threatening. The geographic situation was that Mom and Dad were in Orlando, my sister and her husband were in Houston, and Jim and I were in Nashville. Once again frustrated with the medical community in Orlando, the decision was made to go to M.D. Anderson

Cancer Center in Houston, Texas. The mere fact that a diagnosis had been made and confirmed by other doctors before there was ever a biopsy became a rallying place for our unspent anger. My sister, Melani, and her husband, Dan, lived in Houston, and she became a key player in our family for this new season. She made phone calls, battled prompts and answering machines, faxed, and emailed until she was able to make her way through the barriers of protocol and administration to get Dad an appointment at a cancer hospital before he had any conclusive tests showing his cancer.

I'm reminded that we began to know walking "through the valley of the shadow of death" as a time when we would continually encounter the providential visitations of God's hand. Nurses became angels, doctors became saints, waiting rooms became chapels. If you have the eyes of your heart opened, which an invitation to the Holy Spirit in times of stress can do for you, the view is altogether different from what you anticipated.

The family gathered for Dad's procedure. The doctors would perform a lung biopsy. We all stayed in a one-bedroom apartment down near the hospital. It was a part of the local church's ministry in Houston near the medical centers. They bought condominiums and rented them to families who came to town for various medical treatments at rates that were a fraction of what hotels cost. The waiting list was long, but by an intervening angel we were able to get into one immediately. I wanted to come home and buy all the property near Vanderbilt Hospital and give back the same gift to other people that had been given to us. God does not comfort us to make us comfortable, but to make us comforters (2 Corinthians 1:3-4). Perhaps that was what was happening to us in these early months.

Mel and Dan and Jim and I slept on blow-up mattresses on the floor of the living room. Mom and Dad retreated to the only privacy in the single bedroom. The apartment was eerily silent, except for my brother-in-law's snoring.

I became acquainted with hospital cafeterias and snack bars, waiting rooms and public phones, bathrooms, gift shops, and permitted locations for cell phone use. I encountered the process of illness but refused to look honestly at the possibility of death.

The doctor came out of the surgery to where our little family huddled quietly, nervously laughing at magazine articles or anecdotes, unengaged in anything that stole too much of our attention. The unexpected and welcome report was: "No cancer." After five encounters with people convinced Dad had cancer, it took us a minute to receive this new truth. He had a fungal infection in his lungs that would be difficult to recover from, but he would indeed recover.

We packed up the little apartment, along with our fears of losing Dad, and began to return to where our lives had been a month before. Our relief was almost unreal, the entire experience of the last month an unusual parenthetical phrase in the script of our lives. We turned back to the page where we had left off, the page where Mom was sick and needing better treatment. While we were at M.D. Anderson, our guardian angel, Dr. Radd, a specialist in infectious diseases, arranged for Mom to be seen by a pulmonologist, and the results were that he concurred with the diagnosis from Orlando. He felt that the path of treatment the doctors had Mom on was appropriate, and we began to make peace with that. They would treat Dad's infection, and he would need to return for follow-up appointments in Houston in the fall.

As I read over the words I've written, I'm reminded that the process of losing someone involves so much more than the day they die. It also involves more than the illness itself. The loss and anguish are wrapped in all the infrastructure of family and medical facilities and airlines and careers and rearranging schedules and putting lives on hold and putting friends off and canceling commitments. Not to mention preparing for the inevitability of something so unknown and unknowable as death. Even writing about it now, so soon after Mom's burial, the naked gray trees outside my windows remind me of the bareness of my soul and the naked fears laid open by this experience.

Mom and Dad went home to Orlando. The next six months would be a time of healing for Dad, and a time of rehab for Mom. She drove an hour from her home twice a week for two hours of pulmonary rehab, where they taught her to breathe better. If they could make her breathing more efficient, they could make her life more comfortable. She faithfully did her exercises, and as always with Mom, made friends with the entire rehab staff.

It's funny because even in those six months, I don't know that I ever put my foot down on the ground with confidence that it would hold my weight and not fall out from under me. The long goodbye is a series of ground-lost and ground-gained skirmishes, but it always leaves you in deficit. Every test, every doctor's visit ramps up your emotions with unreasonable expectations. We would live between appointments, hearing, "Things seem good on the blood work. The breathing test was unimproved, but no worse." Devouring any semblance of good news, we broke a little more with each hint at bad news.

Mom and Dad adjusted to life with doctor appointments monopolizing their calendar. Dad regained his strength a little more each day, his hours of sleeping and napping slowly beginning to be less than his hours of waking and functioning. We celebrated Mother's Day, Father's Day, and Mom's birthday, but in a different way than we had the year before. We had met the possibility, the rehearsal for death, and had begun to learn its ways.

# 5

# The News

*The only ultimate disaster that can befall us, I have come*
*to realize, is to feel ourselves at home here on earth.*

MALCOLM MUGGERIDGE

✤

Mom and Dad left Orlando to go to Houston for the follow-up appointment for Dad at Thanksgiving. It seemed unbelievable that it had been a year since Mom's initial diagnosis of pulmonary fibrosis, and six months since Dad's scare with lung cancer. His checkup in Houston showed the good news that his lungs were clean and clear; he was officially released. But they decided to go ahead and have Mom see the pulmonologist again to follow up on her earlier appointments as well. I was surprised because it seemed that they had found a comfortable rhythm with the doctors in Orlando, but Dad was insistent on her seeing this other doctor. The Friday afternoon when my sister called and I asked her how the appointment went, I was barely even engaged. I had been lulled into the season of "maintaining," and I had forgotten how tenuous the body can be. She gave me the news, "Mom has lung cancer," and the breath left my body with no promise of returning. After the preceding year, I just couldn't absorb what she was telling me. I felt like my backyard, which begins to form a lake after a day of rain. The drainage is such that it can't keep up with the falling rain, so the rain collects in a small pond. My ability to absorb bad news was completely gone, and I wept a sorrowful little lake into my hands.

The first time you receive news that your loved one is terminal, or as they now term it, "noncurative," there are no experiences to draw from for coping skills. There is no other disappointment that has ever stolen your mom from you, or your dad, or wife, husband, child, or friend. Death is its own little package of pain, and the only way you learn how to cope is by being there. There are actually studies done about how to deliver bad news. Some will emphasize the importance of environment, that it be comfortable and everyone be on eye level with each other. They stress the importance of the doctor being patient, empathetic, and willing to answer questions. It is suggested to begin by listening, end by summarizing, and agree on a plan. All good things. But nothing makes the news of a loved one's impending death okay. The facts are that with bad news, everyone's life changes. What "was" is over; what "will be" is to be.

Only Holy Spirit presence keeps you from simply folding up your little life and giving up. Only Holy Spirit presence keeps you from screaming and destroying the delicate hope you have rested on. Only Holy Spirit presence sustains you.

I wondered how Jesus felt when He asked for "the cup to pass," and the news from heaven was bad. And how did He feel when Pilate asked the crowd whether to free Him or the notorious criminal Barabbas and the news was bad? When His beloved disciple denied Him three times, how did He feel? He was certainly acquainted with grief and unafraid of the messiness of suffering. He is with me in my sorrow.

Over the next few days, my mind pictured the absolute worst. I think that is how I deal with pain and sorrow. I imagine the worst possible, so that anything else is good news. While the rest of the family were careful to look at one minute at a time, I strained my neck trying to see around the corner, and I mourned the loss of my mother. I would have many opportunities to learn how to best manage this emotional up-and-down experience. This would not be the last time we would receive bad news from a total stranger in a sterile little office. More doctors, more nurses, would be the bearers of bad news. Some were kind, empathetic, even empowering. Some encouraged us beyond our own tired wills. Others would be more passive, protecting themselves from personal involvement under the guise of professionalism, leaving us to manage the new information awkwardly and painfully. I made a mental note for my own experience, to always err on the side of kindness and empathy when sharing bad news with someone. And I tried desperately to effect an even emotional state, refusing the peaks and valleys, preferring to dwell in the flatlands.

Mom would need to have surgery. They would operate to remove the cancerous part of her lung, taking as little as necessary so as not to further exacerbate her already weakened lung condition. She opted to wait until after Christmas, until the first of the year for the surgery, so we could all be together for as normal a holiday as possible. It would be the last Christmas we would share with her.

In the next few weeks, I rolled around in my mind what the news would be after the surgery. Would they be able to get all of the cancer? Would it have spread to her lymph nodes? What stage was the cancer in? I would lie in bed at night, looking through catalogues and imagining what it would be like to not shop for my mother at Christmas, or on Mother's Day, or on her birthday. I wondered what it would be like to not be able to hear her voice on the other end of the phone. I wandered through my memories, celebrating the sweetness of my years with Mom. And I cried.

# 6

# The Shadow of Death

*Even though I walk through the valley of the shadow of death,*
*I fear no evil, for you are with me;*
*your rod and your staff, they comfort me.*

PSALM 23:4 NIV

*Where there is sorrow, there is holy ground.*

OSCAR WILDE

The holidays were bittersweet, with a lot of time spent praying together, touching and holding, crying. We all came to Orlando to celebrate Christmas. The familiar traditions we had shared for so many years at Mom and Dad's home brought comfort to all of us. Mom was determined to cook and keep up, but it was clear that she was sick, and we simplified our routines and ordered out for food when she would let us. We drank deeply of each other's presence.

January 7 was the day surgery was performed to remove part of her lung. The operation was to take place in Houston, so after Christmas Jim and I came back to Nashville first to take care of some details of our life. We then went to Houston with open-ended flight arrangements, unsure of what was ahead of us. Four days after the surgery they gave us the encouraging news that they were able to get all of the cancer, and that it had not spread to any other place. That reality helped us endure weeks of sleepless nights in the hospital because of Mom's unexpectedly severe post-operative pain. Pain management was a disappointing series of failed efforts, but eventually she was well enough to leave, taking with her a new tether to oxygen 24/7. After a several-month recuperation, Mom and Dad were finally able to leave the small apartment they had been staying in near the hospital and return home to Orlando. But she never really got over the surgery.

There were three months of her coughing up blood, and we knew what the doctors in Orlando were too inattentive to notice. It was back. Barely six months after the surgery and the declaration of no cancer, we knew the cancer had returned. The doctors finally tested Mom, and in a dramatic moment they said, "You must rush to Houston for immediate treatment. It doesn't look good." This all less than a week before Mom and Dad's fiftieth wedding anniversary.

Arrangements were made for them to fly immediately. Oxygen was ordered, wheelchairs arranged for, and Jim and I made reservations to meet them in Houston at my sister's home. Two days before their anniversary party, we sat in a cold little examining room at M.D. Anderson and listened to an awkward oncologist tell us that Mom would die in weeks or months without treatment, perhaps a couple of years if all treatment went perfectly. Stunned, we went about taking care of the details for the party, trying to live in a grateful state of the moment.

We had a poignant family gathering there in Houston where Mom and Dad renewed their vows and Jim pronounced them still "husband and wife." Dad kissed his bride through her oxygen tubing, tender and lovingly. Three days later, the radiation treatments started. Five weeks later, it seemed successful in reducing the tumors, but it took a heavy toll. We were told that though the cancer was still present microscopically in her body, they wouldn't treat it until it reared its head. So we carefully rolled Mom out to the car in the wheelchair and lived as if she had a land mine inside of her that might go off at any minute.

She was throwing up a few times each day. Her esophagus was badly burned by the radiation, and her energy was nonexistent. She was in nonstop pain, and the medications to treat it caused her to be more and more absent from us. We were hopeful when she would eat three bites of Jell-O. We watched her weight dwindle. Her immune system was so low that we were on a constant pneumonia watch, even having to rush her to the hospital late at night when her fever spiked and wouldn't drop. My sister's home became a place of caregiving. She, her husband, and my tireless dad attended to Mom's needs at the sacrifice of their own. I commuted back and forth from Nashville to Houston, maintaining a phone vigil in between. I was never completely in either place.

During the season of her treatment, we collected and made memories. I sent care packages from Nashville filled with peppermint lozenges for nausea, nail polish for diversion, and rubber dueling banjo hamsters for laughter. When I was there, after going into town for her doctor appointments, we would eat at drive-through restaurants so Mom wouldn't have to get in and out of the car with her oxygen. We celebrated the day she could eat fried chicken at Popeyes and it didn't hurt her radiation-burned throat. When she was too tired, we ate at home and Mom made a feast out of simple bouillon, exclaiming how wonderful it tasted and how easily it went down. We shopped for some clothes that were comfortable and flattering to her newly reduced figure, and I found myself uttering prayers at the strangest times and for the strangest things. "Let there be a size medium in this beautiful blue velour jacket, Lord. It would really please Mom…thank You!" "God, please let the handicapped dressing room be empty so we can go in and help her try things on…thank You!" "Father, would You just sustain us through this afternoon…thank You." My friend Robert says most prayers are pretty much reduced to one or two words anyway: "Help" or "Thank You."

I flew in at the end of her radiation treatments, but during the three weeks of actual treatment, she, Dad, and my sister had worked out a routine they were comfortable with. The rhythm of disease is awkward, but there is a beat to follow if you listen closely. When I came to be with them, I tried to blend in to the regimen of the morning drive to the hospital. Diet Coke and water in Thermos bags. Moist toilettes for emergency cleanups. Baggies of medications. Oxygen for the drive and more oxygen tanks for walks outside of the van. Pillows to prop up aching limbs. A daily devotional downloaded from the church website to read on the way. They had reinvented normal to bend to the shape of life.

There had been many occasions of sudden throwups, and one morning as we were driving the forty-five minutes in to Houston for Mom's checkup with the radiation doctor, I sat in back with her. I loved it because I could see her face as we sang along to hymns, and I could touch her hand and look into her blue eyes. It came on suddenly. It was my turn. When I saw the obvious signs of what was coming, I tried to grab the small trash can from the rear seat and held it for her so she could throw up. I was choking and heaving and paling, of course all to the hysterical laughter of the rest of the car. Mom was the sick one, and I was the fainting caregiver. Mom laughed and reached for the trash can herself, and while I regained my own stomach, Dad pulled over four lanes of highway traffic to the side of the road and flipped on his emergency flashers. Melani reached for the trash can, opened the door, emptied it, and handed it back. Mom pulled out the wipies, cleaned out the trash can, and put the dirty wipes in a sealed plastic bag. Then we were back on the road as if nothing happened, them functioning as efficiently and quickly as a pit crew. I sipped my Coke and felt ashamed at my frailty, and normal life took on one more different shade.

We sang along to the hymns CD Jim and I had recorded earlier that year. "Blessed assurance...Jesus is mine." We memorized Scripture together: "My soul finds rest in God alone; my salvation comes from him. He alone is my rock and my salvation; he is my fortress, I will never be shaken" (Psalm 62:1-2 NIV). The little white rented minivan became a chapel on wheels.

The thing about the valley of the shadow of death is that I didn't want to walk through it. I didn't want to go through it at all, but I certainly didn't want to walk if I had to pass through there. I wanted to run. I wanted to get it over with as fast as I could and be on the other side. I wanted to scoop Mom up in my arms and race to the other side. The valley was deep, long, and wide, and the other side...well, I couldn't even see it. I knew the Shepherd was with us, that the valley was holy ground. But there was just so much shadow of death.

# 7

# The Dark Night

*The stars are constantly shining, but often we do not see them until the dark hours.*

EARL RINEY

*No matter how deep our darkness—He is deeper still.*

CORRIE TEN BOOM

There was a time when we were told that Mom might have two years if everything went extremely well. I don't know why, but I felt in the quiet of my heart that we would instead be planning a funeral by the end of the year. I don't think I was faithless or maudlin. I think it was just one of those impressions that happens when you are dealing with such delicate matters. I could just as easily have been wrong. And I kept it to myself, except for Jim.

The chronology of this year had been cancer diagnosis in November, surgery in January, recurrence in August, radiation in September, home to Orlando the end of October. November 1, Mom was very sick, but she continued to maintain her amazingly hopeful attitude. She and Dad were trusting the Lord for her days, and they were always careful to reassure us that things

37

were okay. Not great, but okay. They weren't in denial about the underlying realities of what was happening, but they were intentionally making the most of the time. It was less than one year since the initial diagnosis of her cancer. She had been fighting with congestion and coughing for a while, and an on/off fever. This is the rhythm of noncurative disease, of failing health, of dying. There were more sick days than well days. And every new symptom causes you to hold your breath. "Is this it?" This time seemed like the last time the cancer had come back, but it was so soon. Too soon. Surely it wasn't the cancer again.

I was busy with my life, trying to pretend it was my "normal" life. In times like these, you carry around a lead weight of dull sorrow and anticipation and there is no lithe step to your walk, just trudging attempts at pretending you can still live your "normal" life. I was good at busywork and task-oriented assignments. Organizing bookcases, closets, laundry, silverware, flowerpots. Pulling weeds and choosing colors for wall paint. Having lunch with people and engaging in surface chatter. But Mom was dying, and I knew it.

We didn't say that to each other. But we talked several times a day, and unspoken was our need to just hear each other, to be with each other, to memorize each other's presence.

She called on a Tuesday to say that the doctors wanted to check her into the hospital, that she had a bit of pneumonia. But she was absolutely joyous because now, barely over a month since her last radiation treatment, they weren't saying the cancer was back, only pneumonia and they could treat that with three or four days in the hospital. I had been planning to visit within the next two weeks anyway, but I felt compelled to check airline schedules. My sister and her husband were due to arrive there the next day, so I had planned to go later, after they went home.

Still…it felt as though I needed to check airline schedules. So I did.

At lunch the next day, we ate with our dear friends the Alferys. They had lost loved ones to cancer, and he is a doctor; she, a retired nurse. They had been my generous medical consultants and prayerful friends. It's amazing how God plants you in exactly the relationships you need for such a time as this. I told David at lunch what was happening and asked his advice on when I needed to go home. He said it sounded as if she would be okay, and probably I could wait until a little later to go and enjoy a visit. But before we finished lunch, my dad called with the news that Mom was on continuous maximum oxygen and he was concerned. I saw David glance at Joyce, and he said, "I think you need to go now." I knew he was being careful with me. I knew my mom was dying.

That night we would encounter a new level of emotions, fire-filled tears, and moaning because words were insufficient. Months ago we had been told we had maybe two years, and then today, "Oh my, no. Six months at the most," the pulmonologist blurted out. And then that night they said, "She may not make it through the night." I measured the days on the calendar until the end of the year and willed time to wait, feeling more certain of my initial intuition on this point, remembering my feelings that we would lose Mom before the end of the year. I was stranded fourteen hours drive time and twelve hours from my flight time away from my mother. Jim and I lay on the new kitchen floor Mom and Dad had paid for and cried in each other's arms. My spine hurt against the hardwood, but the dimmed lights softened the room. The dogs kept a silent vigil, and as long as the phone didn't ring, I knew Mom was still alive.

I called the junior "Ya-Ya sisters" (Mom had three friends, and they all called themselves the "Ya-Ya sisters," so we referred to my three friends as the junior "Ya-Ya's"), Carm, Deb, and Ev. Each offered their own appropriate brand of comfort; each would have stopped the world for me if they could. I called my cousin Cindy. She loved me through the phone and sobbed her own tears for Mom's pain. My big sister, Melani, was alone with Mom when the doctor said Mom might not make it through the night, and I knew her pain and fear were unbearable burdens. I pictured her by Mom's bedside as the nurses and doctors plied their trade. I pictured her being a five-year-old girl, alone and afraid for her mom. Dad was in the shower at home, forty-five minutes away when he got the call, and my brother-in-law drove him back to the hospital, the tires never touching the ground. I sipped some mulled wine and held my legs close to my chest, and the only prayer I knew to pray for the moment was, "Lord, have mercy. Christ, have mercy."

What other words signify the desire for God to be God, for Him to see all and manage it in His godlike wisdom? What is more eloquent and complete than "Lord, have mercy"?

I would endure a mostly sleepless night, the darkest night I could remember. I wondered if the rest of the world was sleeping. I kept my cell phone, Jim's cell phone, and our house phone beside the bed and lay there under the glow of cable news. I didn't dare wish for morning, unsure of what the light would reveal. And somewhere around 4 A.M., the night wrapped its darkness around me and I surrendered to a fitful sleep.

# 8

# The Goodbye

*All of us must die eventually. Our lives are like water spilled out*
*on the ground, which cannot be gathered up again.*
*That is why God tries to bring us back when we have*
*been separated from him.*
*He does not sweep away the lives of those he cares about...*

2 SAMUEL 14:14 NLT

❧

The next morning I called my sister, and she said Mom had made it through the night and was a little more stabilized. We gathered our bags, packed with dark suits just in case, and left for the airport. We had a nonstop flight, and I cocooned myself under eyeshaders and behind earplugs, snuggling next to the cold hard steel wall of the plane that would deliver me to my mother's bedside. We landed and unloaded our only bags from the overhead compartment, and then dragged them in silence to the shuttle that took us to the terminal and my brother-in-law waiting at the curbside. We drove the forty-five minutes to the hospital, discussing our frustration with the doctors, aiming our anger at something. When we got to the hospital, we became "those people" with glazed faces, suffering the unknown pain of anticipated loss in a hospital intensive care waiting room. We became those people I've always felt sorry for and prayed God's comfort for. We were the ones wringing our hands outside the nurses' station, carefully weighing every action that went on behind Mom's pulled curtain. We were a healthy family not so long ago, and now we were unbelievably those people preparing to say goodbye. It just wasn't real.

We could only go in to see Mom one or two at a time. Jim and I instantly noted how beautiful she looked, soft and feminine, blue eyes bright and staring through my soul. She was cheerful, as she always was, and said, "Hello there, Jim Thomas!" through a mask blowing oxygen loudly into her lungs, and she reached for and squeezed my hand. Hers was soft and smooth like satin, and I tenderly held it with both of mine. We spoke of God's faithfulness. We talked about Dad being tired, and she told me how pretty I looked. I wept a tiny bit and bent over to hug her. "Why do I love you so much?" she would say. " 'Cause I'm your angel," I would dutifully reply. It was our little script throughout my childhood.

When your mother is dying, I thought you would feel helpless and small. Days later when she did leave us, I did feel small, but not now. Now I felt big, and adrenaline moved me through the day. I wanted to swallow her up in my arms, protect her, deny death its opportunity to find her. I felt like the angel in Rodin's *La Defence,* fiercely battling anyone trying to come after the wounded one lying in my arms.

Maybe that is also the picture of our heavenly Father caring for us. As I was holding Mom, He was holding both of us. He would carry Mom from my arms to heaven. And all the while, still hold me.

For the next hour I was privileged to sit with her. I read her some psalms, and she slept a bit. At one point, after she had rested, I asked her if she was afraid. Without a pause she said, "No, honey. I'm not afraid. Not afraid of death. Maybe a little afraid of the pain." And I begged God in that exact moment to protect her from the pain, and I thanked Him for her amazing courage and thoughtfulness to reassure me of her faith. As I look back, this was one of the most important conversations we had. It silently acknowledged that we both knew she was dying; we were not unaware of the reality we were moving toward. It gave us each a chance to then say we loved each other in a different way. In a grateful way.

But that day hope was changing, adapting again. The hope of her going back to her house had to be let go of. The new hope was for a good night's rest, less pain, a deep breath. The old hope was for things to be the way they were before. The new hope was for things to be the way they are promised to be.

The time passed with trips to the Coke machine, swabbing Mom's dry lips with ice, rubbing her forehead. I had books to read, but I couldn't concentrate past a few words. The television offered some distraction, but it was hard to stay with a story, or care about the commercials, or be involved in the world at large. Our world had become a small cosmos of hospital room, cafeteria, chapel, and elevator. I walked the halls in search of any sleeping endorphins, and I just kept praying, "Lord, have mercy. Christ, have mercy."

The honest truth is that I came to the end of myself hourly. If I let my mind focus on the absolute sorrow of losing Mom, I started down a spiral I couldn't recover from. So I didn't let myself go there. I recited Scripture verses of reassurance as they would come to my mind, which most of the time felt as though it were on pause. I found I couldn't ask for anything specific from God. I couldn't ask for more time, for wisdom, for anything but mercy. I was coming to understand that in the most critical passages of life, I honestly wanted to trust God to make the decisions, to see everything and put it all together the best way. I was afraid I would do or want or ask for less than His best design for that moment.

The reserves we draw from in these times are deep and endless. They are the reality of the promises. They are the unfamiliar territory that quickly becomes familiar. They are the small candles in the shadows. They are a cold Diet Coke, a hot egg-and-cheese biscuit sandwich from McDonald's, a soft pillow for fifteen minutes, a smile on Mom's face after a nap. Most of all they are the silent assurances from the Spirit that peace is being offered.

Peace is passed to our hearts even in the ceaseless emotion, the waves of panic, the sleepless nights. Those next days would bring deeply sorrowful times. Watching my dad come to grips with the fact that his soul mate would not be coming home again. Seeing the two of them resolutely choose against life support. Noticing the real "Mom" slip under a current of drugs that were to comfort her but stole her true presence from us with each drip into her veins. One night Jim and I would go back to Mom and Dad's house, and I would walk in to see the last day she had been there. Perfume still uncapped, freshly washed lingerie pinned up in the laundry room, meat thawed for a future dinner, flowers waiting to be watered. Life waiting for Mom to come home. But she wouldn't.

After several nights that were only worth remembering because of the quiet singing Jim and I stereophonically whispered into Mom's ears, recanting the *Agnus Dei* melodies and lyrics of promise and comfort, I was walking numb. I didn't sleep, but more often tried to huddle my legs under my rear end (which there was daily less of) like a hen on eggs. The Band-Aid pink

room with fluorescent lighting gave no illusion of home or comfort, and the full cans of Ensure that Mom so diligently drank at
each meal were lingering testimony to her progressive slide away
from us. The LED readouts to the right of her head incessantly
beeped out their codes of warning and prohibition. The small
solo monitor on the table that measured the amount of oxygen
Mom was getting in her blood buzzed us into a ragged state, and
we unplugged it with the approval of the night nurse.

Mom would hum songs with us and we would recite her
favorite Scriptures: "My soul finds rest in God alone; my salvation
comes from him. He alone is my rock and my salvation; he is my
fortress, I will never be shaken" (Psalm 62:1-2 NIV). The words
of the psalmist that have sustained us for months. We would hold
hands, and under the candle glow of morning, she would turn
like a page into the waking hands of heaven.

The peace was thin as a spider's skein; it was hard to imagine
it would hold. But it continually did. I wanted her to be completely peaceful and comfortable, not involved in another fight,
even the struggle of death. I wanted her to slip away painlessly
with no marks or bruises from this horrible intruder.

Perhaps that is exactly how it was from behind her skin. Perhaps. I felt that there was a presence of Knowing, and that Mom
was not afraid. But her unrest, her struggle, her compressed eye-
brows that spoke of pain did not match the picture I had in my
mind. I squeezed her hand and begged God for His promise of
comfort and peace, dropping my tears on Mom's blanket where
she wouldn't see. She didn't squeeze back anymore. She was only
barely in our world with us; she was more in another world that
I would not be able to walk beside her in. In those long hours, I
desperately wanted for her to sit up and be Mom again. But as the

night lingered, I silently allowed for my heart to mouth words that longed for her to pass.

In one particularly fitful bout, she restlessly pulled off her oxygen mask, pushed off her covers, pulled at her IVs, verbally thrashed the nurses and breathing therapist. I fought with her to keep her mask on—she "must have it on to get any air"—and I tried to console her inconsolable tender heart, telling her that I loved her. She said, "No, you don't, or you would get me out of here." I nervously tried to gather the broken parts of my heart before she could see them, and I stroked her head saying, "I know, Mom. It's okay."

The increased agitation from the decreased oxygen in her body was becoming harder to see past. I knew this was the drugs and rumors of a failing body speaking, not the sweet mother I had always known and who diligently encouraged and loved every attendant who walked through her door this past week. To get to the "incorruptible," you have to trade in the "corruptible."

"Faith is the assurance of things hoped for, the conviction of things not seen" (Hebrews 11:1). What I saw was my very vulnerable mom, clothed in paper-thin skin from months of steroids, straining for air. Tubes of medicine, external veins of failing use, hung from hooks tangling Mom to her earthly body. A mask forced oxygen through her nose and open mouth like a small hurricane of life. Her chest had long since tired, and now her diaphragm was heaving at a rate I couldn't match with my own breathing. The heart monitor screamed beeps, indicating her heart rate was over 130 beats a minute, and yet I was sure, or as close to sure as you can be in those kind of moments, that what He promised, He would do. Deep behind the suffering that God allowed for my benefit, so that I would begin to let go of her, down where the real Mom was that I couldn't see, she was at peace and not suffering. Down there, there were no beeps and alarms, no heaving chests or lungs, no racing heartbeats. Just because I couldn't see it didn't mean it wasn't her reality. While I held her smooth and nonresponsive hands, the hands of her soul were held by the Comforter who told her not to fear and promised that the waves wouldn't overwhelm her and the flames wouldn't burn her (Isaiah 43:2). The psalmist said that His rod and staff would comfort her, and in the book of Lamentations we are assured that His compassions and mercies would never fail her (Lamentations 3:22).

At 7:15 on Thursday morning, November 13, 2003, Mom graduated to heaven. Her earthly vessel lay unearthly still, and her spirit was absent from it, present with the Lord. Joyful for her home going, broken by the separation, we all held hands around her and cried through peaceful smiles.

# 9

# The Mourning After

*But we do not want you to be uninformed, brethren,*
*about those who are asleep, so that you will not grieve*
*as do the rest who have no hope.*

1 THESSALONIANS 4:13

❧

I told my young friend four years ago when her father died that death is a thief and grief is a bully. Now the thief and bully have taken up residence in my life, and I am trying to make room for them. Mourning has me weaving between feelings of guilt over my sadness and feelings of confidence in the providence of God's eternal now, and I come up next to sorrow that threatens to choke off my air. Again I find there are no instructions for this experience, no directions for the mourner's path.

The day Mom died, we all went back to the house in two cars, Dad's car and Mom's car. We got busy doing what we knew how to do. It was better to be doing than sitting and thinking or feeling. My sister and I cleaned out the obvious reminders of Mom: her oxygen, medicines, clothes, and makeup. We went through the refrigerator and threw out things past expiration dates, signs of Mom's decreasing ability to keep up with the house. And then we came on a can of black-eyed peas in the pantry. One can. Just enough for our first meal after her passing. She had been famous in our family for being able to make a party out of a can of black-eyed peas. When things were slow because of low money or low activity, Mom would get a big grin on her face, clap her hands, and say, "Let's have black-eyed peas and cornbread!" And suddenly things were okay, and the enjoyment of simple things became a party. So that day, the day of her heavenly party, we heated her very personal party tools, and each of us made our own plate with black-eyed peas and cornbread, and ate in the silence of our grief and memories. Dad ate with a phone to his ear; my brother-in-law ate with a notepad, getting a start on funeral plans; Melani ate as she cleaned the kitchen; Jim ate by the computer; and I ate at the table. The spirit of Mom was with each of us. The Spirit of God held us all together.

The next days were filled with the duties of closing down a life. I was privileged to write Mom's obituary, in a state of suspended belief that the words I was writing were actually about my own mom. Decisions on caskets, flowers, location for services, who would be involved. In the greater context of eternity, of heaven, which is where we had to be to find any comfort, things like which kind of casket seemed irrelevant and tedious. The symbols and props of packaging death in the most lovely of pictures are still horrendous in an unspoken way. Putting makeup on an empty face, dressing the body in favorite clothes. Spraying familiar perfume so that Mom's scent was present. There is a macabre tone I struggled to get past. We all knew the earthly housing of Mom was retired from use; she would not be needing it in her new home. That she was not present in that carefully presented body. But these are some of the tools of early grief, helping us make the passage from disbelief to reality. Touching her hands that were now cold and hard sealed the fact that she was not there, sleeping in front of us. The choices were another way to honor Mom, one last way to connect. And that was important. So a beautiful "Ann blue" casket was selected, modestly lovely like Mom, and red roses were chosen, a love language between her and Dad.

The memorial service was held four days later, at First Baptist in Orlando. Family and friends came; hundreds filed through the chapel. As Dad had so wanted, it was truly a celebration, both of Mom's life and her home going. If you've ever wondered if sending flowers gives any comfort to the family, it does indeed. We had put the word out for people wanting to send something to make a donation to a fund at Campus Crusade for Christ that would be used in a way that honored Mom. But several people sent flowers anyway, and they were a help in the celebration. My sister and I each wore a set of Mom's pearls, and I wore a blouse in her favorite shade of blue. We came to call blue-sky days "Ann blue" skies over that next week. Photos, favorite songs, and favorite verses were a part of the service. The truth and hope of the gospel were presented as Mom had wanted, and a few of us shared personal remembrances. Gwen, Ella, and Mary, Mom's Ya-Ya's, brought their Ya-Ya hats and shared fun stories. I told of Mom's hands, that squeezed "I love you," applauded my accomplishments and attempts, led me to Jesus, folded to pray, packed up my childhood, and set another plate at the table for my husband. We thanked God that we do not sorrow as people without hope because of the promise of heaven, which looks brighter and more desirable now that Mom is there. It isn't that the joy of Christ in heaven isn't enough. It's just that knowing Mom is there gives the abstract idea a little more reality.

I tried to picture what heaven is like, and what level of awareness those who have gone before us have. I'm not sure of the answers to those questions. The mystery is deep. But I think that because time is not linear in God's eyes, maybe where Mom is, we are all there with her. In "chronos," God's time, the eternal now of heaven, there is no measurable distinction between the time of her death and ours, and all things are fulfilled and redeemed where she is. It's abstract, and mostly unknowable, but it gives me comfort.

Mel and Dan are back in Houston, Dad is in Orlando, Jim and I are in Nashville. We are all trying to find the path we are to walk in this season. It is a mourner's walk. When people ask how he is doing, Dad says his best answer is, "I am mourning." There is no right amount of time for it, no right pattern, no right way to feel. It is just a new reality that comes when we walk here. There is a dullness, and then an acute sharpness when you feel too much. There are moments of confusion, and some of painful clarity. We don't deny God's faithfulness, but the pain is distinctly present. I find I can thank God for the fact that Mom is in heaven, that her suffering is over, that He will take care of us and our pain. But I can't thank Him for the separation. Because that's not how He ever wanted it to be either. That is why Jesus wept at Lazarus' tomb. The cost of sin was death, separation from God. Even Jesus experienced that agony on the cross. And every separation we experience aches because it is not the way it was supposed to be. Thank God for His Son, making a way to reunite us, and us with Mom. It is the reality I know, the conviction of what I can't see yet.

So I am trying. It is a choice to choose faith over sight. When I choose to believe what I can't see, faith is birthed in a new room of my heart. I have emptied that room to leave plenty of space for the impending arrival of all that faith. It is the spare room, next door to the room where the thief and the bully will be staying for an undetermined length of time.

# The Healing

# 10

# Two Months Later

*Come to the edge He said. They said: We are afraid.*
*Come to the edge He said.*
*They came. He pushed them, and they flew...*

GUILLAUME APOLLINAIRE

❧

*I*t is two months after Mom's death, and it is difficult for me to even consider the process of healing right now. The cynic in me that is afraid to hope again has a hold on my heart and feeds gluttonously on her hurt. The pain is so consistently with me that I'm not sure I can let go of it, because I'm afraid I will have to begin to let go of Mom. I am sure I want to be more well than I am right now. I want to know the sweetness of each day and the anticipation of goodness. I want to mourn and recover. To throw myself back into the possibilities of life, still loving Mom.

As the details of closure are completed and there are less and less tangible responsibilities to fill my days, I am more and more contemplative. I am considering the business of death, the application of loss to my life. And I am considering the steps involved in healing, recovering from the mourner's season.

I know there are books to be written, paintings to be painted, relationships to tend. They have all been on hold, and I need to pay attention again. It's just that it seems almost disrespectful to write or paint or have lunch with friends. It seems unfair to heal now. Mom has died, and everything from this point forward is different.

I want to be whole. To be okay again. But it feels as though if I'm okay again, then I will have forgotten Mom or I will somehow have carelessly treated her memory. I have a driving need to always find the "best way" to handle anything in life. I weigh options and ask opinions and pray for inspiration. If there are scriptural applications, I get a concordance and search. My perfectionist DNA forces me to know there is a "best way" to do anything. To open a can, to fold a towel, to deal with grief. This tendency threatens any possibility of healthy progression in my mourning. I'm afraid of being an unfaithful pilgrim if I acknowledge the doubts and uncertainties that have challenged my spiritual convictions. I'm afraid to put my full weight down on my faith in a place I've never had to. What if it doesn't hold? And is it unfaithful of me to even ask that? So if I don't know the best way to be faithful, I'll just do nothing. As much as I want to hope, that feels tenuous and uncertain too. Will I just be hurt and haunted by things that will only disappoint me again? But if I don't risk hope, will I become bitter and hard? And if I am vulnerable to the actual pain of this separation from Mom, will it go deeper and take more of me?

Jim says that there isn't always a "best way" for every situation in the strictest philosophical sense. After we argued the point to exhaustion, the two of us arguing uncharacteristic sides of the issue, I think I understand his thoughts, and I might even agree. It is partly a semantics issue, but even more it is a heart-set issue.

There is truth, knowable and unchanging truth, about the foun-dational issues of life and faith, and there are irrefutable facts of science. But there are *more* mysteries than there are facts. Which means there are more "better ways" than "best ways."

I am told that a skin wound begins the healing process from the bottom up and from the outer edges of the wound inward. Certainly this happens after the hemorrhaging has stopped. The flow of blood has to be temporarily halted to this section of the body until initial stages of healing are in place. As connective tissue expands in the wounded area, a foundation is laid for new skin that will once again thrive with a network of blood vessels facilitating the blood supply. The initial flush is a bearable loss as the blood typically cleanses the wound, taking with it any foreign matter that might cause infection later.

I have experienced a gash to my emotional world. Not to mention the gaping hole left in my physical existence where Mom used to stand. If I don't find myself at least trying some of the better options for beginning the healing process, the essence of my life will bleed out until I have no energy to put toward repair. I'll need to put some pressure on the wound, as much as it doesn't feel right. Some pressure to try again. I will begin from the bottom up, and from the outer edges in. Perhaps if I allow myself to do this better than I did yesterday, I will one morning find myself in the middle of healing.

# 11

# Faith

*Faith is daring the soul to go beyond what the eyes can see.*

J.R.R. TOLKIEN

*So we fix our eyes not on what is seen, but on what is unseen.*
*For what is seen is temporary, but what is unseen is eternal.*

2 CORINTHIANS 4:18 NIV

When a young friend asked me if the process of losing my mom caused me to doubt my faith, I paused before trying to answer. I didn't want, in any way, to threaten her own delicate faith, but I knew she would see through anything but my most honest response. The truth was that there were indeed times when I was pleading with God to be what I wanted, my definition of real and caring. "Is this all just smoke and mirrors?" passed for prayer sometimes. Through clouded eyes in waiting rooms I screamed in my mind, *Have I bought the grandest lie of history, that there is a God who cares for us?*

I don't think God was offended by my prayers. Even praying through the veil of doubt is the beginning of faith. There was

59

never really a time I can say that I didn't believe in God, but there were deep wells of doubt as to whether He was paying attention and was indeed working all things to our good. It would seem that it is better to let those feelings out, rather than lock them away to rust my soul.

During many restless nights in Mom's hospital room, I was distinctly aware that living in the seen/unseen world is the paradox of faith. The things I saw did not convince me of the comfort promised by my loving heavenly Father. And the sentimentality of hollow platitudes were not enough to sustain my family. Faith had to become more than words I had read, more than a cross-stitched pillow, more than a concept of undefinable distinction. It was becoming the conviction of seasoned and tried believers, and it ebbed and flowed.

In the hospital, the helplessness was sometimes overwhelming. If faith wasn't found where I was looking, I looked somewhere else. Small victories took the shape of miracles that God allowed to build and support our fragile faith. A breathing mask that the respiratory therapist created from two other masks was less uncomfortable, less claustrophobic, and so we gave thanks. They served chocolate-flavored Ensure for lunch, Mom enjoyed it, and it became manna, enough provision for the need of the moment. Getting her pillows all lined up to support her head and back just right was a momentary expression of God's presence in the middle of so much need. These small epiphanies of comfort began to build my trust in the unseen, and faith would swell and fill my heart.

At other times, when the fiercely constant presence of God was unseen, it was felt. I barely made it through the second hand ticking past each number on the clock some hours, watching Mom in such discomfort, agitated by lack of oxygen. There was a consuming darkness and the shadow of death was foreboding. But even in the deficit of immediate answers to prayer, the intense promise of heaven and the immutable Presence pierced the dark. I was weak; He was strong. I was frail, faint, and failing. He was limitless, unending, and relentless. I was living in a thin place, where the realities of earth and heaven are almost merged, where the comfort of the unseen is almost seen, and where faith becomes palpable currency.

Those were the times when even through the haze of drugs, Mom would sometimes open her eyes and squeeze my hand, and just for a moment, it was the way it used to be. We would look into each other's eyes, and then she would go back to sleep, back to the place I couldn't see.

After Mom died, in the pit of my sorrow, sometimes down in that well of doubt, there were days when I didn't want to leave my bed. Jim would consistently and tenderly invite me to get dressed and go for a walk with him. We would start the walk at a brisk pace, sometimes in silence, him allowing me time to wake up and make my decision to be present, to trust for today. Within a few blocks, the astonishing efficiency of muscle and sinew and bone coordinating to move my body forward was its own affirmation of God's presence, and the sky would ring with relevance, and the order of creation would speak of an ordered Designer, and everything would be reduced to its foundation again. In observing the creation around me, my awareness of God in the seen world reinforced my assurance of God in the unseen world. The first cause to all that exists, a Designer behind the design, settled the restlessness in my heart, in the well of doubt. And at the bedrock where I had been holding my breath, my faith that God was aware of our suffering and able to shepherd us through this time would surface once again.

Faith is not easy, neat, or safe. Death is certainly a challenge to the tidy picture of simplistic faith. I even wonder if faith can be reckoned to a person until it has been challenged in the crucible of sorrow.

There have been moments of heroic faith and times of childish unfaithfulness. But faith is not about "beating cancer" or "cheating death." At the risk of sounding brash, that is wishful thinking. Faith that has taken up residence in my heart looks more like surrender, trust that a loving Father will show mercy in the way that maintains our highest good. It is a gift that is given by the Holy Spirit, and by the grace of God, not something I must work up on my own. If that results in "beating cancer" or "cheating death," it is not because I believed it, but because God willed it. And in the same way, though Mom did not "beat cancer" and did not experience total healing in the way I would have liked, that does not indicate a faulty faith in an unable God. The fact that she was rescued from this earth and ushered through death's door into the arms of God is the unseen conviction of my faith. The "seen" part is that my family and I have been sustained through the valley of the shadow of death and come out the other side still trusting, one minute at a time.

That's what I tried to share with my young friend as we sat on the patio of Baja Burrito. I'm not sure there was much eloquence or beauty to my answer, or even satisfaction for her question. But I hope that when she next encounters suffering of any magnitude, she will remember and hold on, while the certain and unseen God authors faith enough for her journey in her heart, as He did and is doing in my own.

12

# Hope

*Hope is anticipation of good not yet here, or as yet "unseen."*
DALLAS WILLARD

*Hope is faith holding out its hands in the dark.*
GEORGE ILES

*It is the difference between paint, which is merely laid on the surface, and a dye or stain which soaks right through.*

C.S. LEWIS

Dad called from his home in Orlando this morning. It was unusually cold here in Nashville for this time of year, morning indistinguishable from afternoon by its overcast heaviness. I was writing upstairs, so I had unplugged the phone, but I overheard the answering machine downstairs. I could tell it was Dad's voice on the other end, and it sounded somber. Different from sad. I tried to call back right then but got no answer, so I decided he probably got Jim on his cell phone. A quick call to Jim got no answer and confirmed my suspicion.

I tried to eat some Frosted Mini-Wheats with skim milk and pay attention to the morning cable news. But I felt a familiar swell of dread rising in my stomach the way the ocean rises off the floor when a swollen wave is about to slam the shore.

When Jim finally called me back, before I even got to "hello," I said, "What's wrong with Dad?" Jim's recollection was scattered, and it wasn't until another hour later when Dad called back that I got the full story. It seems he had been to see the eye specialist about a rescheduled cataract procedure and in the process they discovered there was pressure on his optical nerve. I listened, and with every breath, every nuance of word, I tried not to go months down the road of fear. Familiar adrenaline stimulated the flight or fight response, and my heart pounded in my ears. The pressure, when coming from the exterior, is an indicator of glaucoma, an incurable disease that can end in blindness if they don't arrest it quickly. A quick Google search told me that it is treatable, and while they can't recover any lost vision, they can usually slow the progression. But the pressure on Dad's optical nerve was coming from the interior, which is not usual, and it could indicate a tumor. An MRI was scheduled for Monday.

Jim and I walked over to the International Market Restaurant a couple of blocks from our home, and I cried while we held hands. I felt like a fraud for feeling the fear and anxiety I was feeling. Hadn't I learned anything over this last year? These tears sting the same way the ones did that I cried over Mom's initial diagnosis last November. This time there was no confirmed diagnosis yet, and indeed Dad's condition may turn out to be entirely treatable. But that is the hard part about losing your innocence. This year I have become more acquainted with the ravages of this failing creation, and I am aware that sickness and death are inevitabilities, costs of the Fall. I am afraid to hope.

Mom's death has marked in bold letters across my childish hope, "DECLINED," and I am just now starting to see those letters fade in deference to the promises of God. I have only recently begun to regather my willingness to allow for the expectation of future good, pausing to confirm the honesty of each anticipation. I can see that my childish hope sat on the surface and peeled at the first sign of rain. I have had to scrape the peeling paint, to unmask the rawness, before I can apply a fresh coat of new hope. I've had to expose the impostors that masqueraded as a bankable future but denied the reality of death. I thought that if I just didn't dwell on it, I wouldn't have to deal with it. That's a tidy little life that doesn't hold up under the reality of suffering. It's as plausible as my husband's little brother, who used to think that if he closed his eyes, you couldn't see him.

Maturing hope makes peace with the inevitability of death. It isn't a soulless resignation of "dust to dust" that slips slowly into nihilism. There is a beauty for ashes promised. There is a blessedness promised to the mourner. There is a logical progression that allows for my suffering to bring about a hope that "does not disappoint" (Romans 5:5). And there is an ultimate assurance that we do not sorrow without hope, because Christ has made heaven sure for us. There is a mystical already-but-not-yet kingdom where God has made all things new and whole. He has set things as they were intended to be, and Mom is there, and I will see her again. I don't know what it looks like, and what state she is in now. I imagine, admittedly with little scriptural support, that Mom is experiencing the fullness of time in the eternal now. We are all together where she is. What is "yet to come" for me is "already" where she is. I know there is no sadness; Scripture does tell me that about heaven. The hope of her being totally as God intended her to be and experiencing the mysteries of heaven, and the promise that we will join her there one day, is the most sustaining hope I have right now.

These are indeed the makings of real hope to be collected and planted in my heart. And whatever the situation is with Dad's health now, I will need that hope, and so will he. The plantings are just seedlings, vulnerable to more news of tragedy or trial, and I just need a little time, and a little shade. Time for roots to grow deep and strong, shade from the heat of new stress. This is the care that the Father promises to give in Psalm 121, care that will protect my hope.

*I will lift up my eyes to the mountains;*
*from whence shall my help come?*
*My help comes from the LORD, who made heaven and earth.*
*He will not allow your foot to slip;*
*He who keeps you will not slumber.*
*Behold, He who keeps Israel will neither slumber nor sleep.*
*The LORD is your keeper; the LORD is your shade on your right hand.*
*The sun will not smite you by day, nor the moon by night.*
*The LORD will protect you from all evil; He will keep your soul.*
*The LORD will guard your going out and your coming in*
*from this time forth and forever.*

PSALM 121

# 13

# *S*urrender

*Oh, I come to you with a message, fearful and anxious one.*
*God does not ask you to give the perfect surrender in your strength,*
*or by the power of your will; God is willing to work it in you.*

ANDREW MURRAY

*I must be ploughed up and resown.*

C.S. LEWIS

❦

There is a natural tendency to resist the pain of this season. I find I would rather be filled with concrete than blood, so that I can't bleed anymore, feel anymore.

The safety of retreat calls to me in a voice disguised as comfort, and I have cloistered myself some, looking for rest. But I know that eventually retreat becomes denial, which doesn't yield wellness. And there is another voice that whispers to me. It entices me to aim my disappointment in a blade of anger at whatever is closest. And I have done that a little bit too. I've been angry at doctors for being less than I expect of them, for not handling carefully the fragile life of my mother. I've spent some unhealthy hours in retreat and in anger—usually because I have been frustrated at how much is out of my control.

I had no control over the number of Mom's days. I couldn't will it, fix it, or buy it. I couldn't be good enough or smart enough or clever enough to steal days away from death for her. I couldn't even pray the right prayer or meditation that would control God's design for my mom's life. I didn't like this reality, and I found surrender a most difficult experience. Having convinced myself that I had control of a lot of my life, and having the nervous stomach condition to prove how earnest my efforts were, I find surrender unnatural for me. I've grown up studying hard enough and putting in enough effort to get an "A" most of the time, enough of the time that I learned a "cause and effect" approach that has proved to be inaccurate in the reality of much of life's more important situations. As much as I have an artist's heart, I have the mind of someone who needs to see around corners, to anticipate and control.

Mom, on the other hand, suffered in grace. I watched her choose to fight what she could and then surrender to what was out of her control. The sovereignty of God was the net beneath all of her efforts. She and Dad had found a place of surrender to God's plan that actually strengthened them. There was never any giving up or resignation. I saw strength that carried them through constant setbacks.

The night this past summer when we found out Mom's cancer was back after her surgery, I went to bed with such heaviness, such frustration at this disease so out of our control. As hard as we fought, as Mom fought, the disease fought harder and more aggressively. While I tossed in bed that night, a delicate rain fell. The next morning, the smell of earth was quietly pungent, invading my nostrils as I opened the back door to call the dogs

in from their morning excursion through the garden and sur-
rounding areas of the backyard. There was freshly turned soil in
the part of the garden I worked in yesterday, and steam lifted
from its surface, fading like a memory less than two feet from
where it began.

On this wet morning, I went out to work for just a while in
the cool of the early hours. The busyness would be cathartic, a
healthy distraction from the other things on my mind. The
garden was so overrun by weeds I had a hard time finding my
original plantings. The weeds surrendered to my hand easily, and
before the sun began to bake everything, I carted a small heap to
the mulch pile.

The skin of earth beneath the southwestern corner maple had
caught my eye for the patterning that had developed on the surface. The rain had come and then drained well beneath the surface, leaving a scab of sun-baked earth. The mud had surrendered
its form to the shape of the roots, and to the rocks, which were
barely hidden below the surface like little mounds and hiccups.
Naked of grass or weeds, the mud signaled to me a bravery as it
sat bare and available for future deposits.

This season of tears has rained hard on my heart, and its
freshly turned ground is indeed naked and bare. I long to signal
it to surrender, conforming to the presence of the Spirit hovering
just below the surface, over the darkness of my sadness. I want to
bravely give my soul up to new plantings, surrendering the weeds
of summer without struggle.

Surrender will mean letting go of what wasn't intended to be
mine in the first place. It's just so hard to give up control. Control of how things will be, how things should be, how I will make
them be. God gives us dignity by allowing our participation in
some areas of our life, but the absolute surrender He asks of us

leaves no room for my insistence of control. The week my mom's health decidedly turned, my friend Dr. David said to me, "Kim, you are upset because you think last week you had everything under control. But any illusion you had of that was simply that, an illusion."

The need to control, to know "why, God, did You let this happen," wears deeply into my reserves of wellness. And the slavery of sadness is heavy. I know that surrendering my feelings of anger, control, resentment, disappointment, and fear is not a reticent act of "losing." It is unparalleled freedom from the burden of being in charge. It has little to do with visible effort and everything to do with interior cultivation. Quiet renovations of soul and spirit. There aren't three easy steps, or seven surefire methods, or any quick paths to surrender. It is a process of trial and error, surrendered ground, lost ground, and surrendered again.

As I put away the tools in my gardening basket that night, I took off my suede utility gloves and laid them in the pile. Constant use had caused them to conform to the shape of my hand, and they sat eerily sculptural, having surrendered their form to mine. I prayed a silent vespers prayer that I would do the same. I would surrender my ways to His.

# 14

# *The Comfort of Friends*

*Blessed be the God and Father of our Lord Jesus Christ,*
*the Father of mercies and God of all comfort,*
*who comforts us in all our affliction so that we may be able*
*to comfort those who are in any affliction*
*with the comfort with which we ourselves are comforted by God.*

2 CORINTHIANS 1:3-4

*Those who are not afraid to hold a hand in gratitude,*
*to shed tears in grief,*
*and to let a sigh of distress arise straight from the heart can*
*break through paralyzing boundaries and witness*
*the birth of a new fellowship, the fellowship of the broken.*

HENRI NOUWEN

When Jesus went to the Garden to pray the night before His passionate pilgrimage of suffering, He didn't go alone. The Gospel of Matthew records that the disciples went with Him. Once they got to Gethsemane, it tells us that He took three of them with Him to a quiet place of prayer, and began to be "troubled and sorrowful." Even Jesus wept in the company of friends.

Empathetic friends with whom I can be "troubled and sorrowful" have been a necessary part of holding me together this year. The comfort has been immediate as their concern transformed the loneliness of sorrow into the intimacy of a shared journey. There have been friends who both pursued and received my tearful calls, some of them crying with me, others encouraging me that they love me and Mom. Some who have walked the mourner's path have given me tools that were helpful to them, sharing them with the wisdom and warmth of experience.

I have been grateful for the support of those who love me and have let me muddle my way through on occasion. They haven't rushed me to wholeness without allowing the natural process of healing to happen. Even those who were less sensitive, saying the wrong thing, reaching for clichés that actually hurt more than help, were surely well intentioned, just trying to love me in their own awkward way. I learned that to sit quietly with someone's tears, to mend them gently, to sit with the sorrowful and be patient with their pain, is a gift of immeasurable value.

After Mom's death, her friends and fellow sojourners in Orlando poured out their care and concern for our family. Men came and sat quietly in the living room or on the porch with Dad, allowing him to tell the story and heal a little with each visit. Women who loved Mom brought food and tender hugs. Especially her Ya-Ya's, who were there the first night and every day after. We didn't go a day without someone from Mom and Dad's Sunday school class or Campus Crusade for Christ, where they had served together for a dozen years, coming by with gifts of food. I had never understood the ministry of "withness" that food provides. It was the perfect way of saying "we are with you" and providing for a basic need. People brought chickens, ham, casseroles, salads, disposable dinner plates, cups, and silverware. Some brought basic groceries like milk, bread, and eggs so that we wouldn't have to think about those things. Once they discovered our love of Diet Cokes and Arizona Diet Green Tea, the refrigerator and coolers stayed full. Calls came in asking if we needed sweets or treats, vegetables or fruits. Not only was all of this provision generous expressions of care, it also filled the huge hole that Mom always filled in the kitchen. And it said we weren't alone.

Hundreds came to the funeral, and each one came up and hugged or simply touched Dad, and honored Mom with words of remembrance. Their presence filled the room and the emptiness. Campus Crusade provided a reception after, where we could comfortably visit and even share laughter to mend the wounds. Friends of mine flew from Nashville and drove from Tampa. I was silenced by their generosity.

Almost a month later, the Ya-Ya's even flew up to Washington, D.C., for Mom's burial at Arlington Cemetery, and we shared tears and joyful brownies in the warmth of a cozy coffee shop. Jim's family patiently and quietly supported us with their loving presence. And while we were gathering at Arlington Cemetery, I turned around to see my best friend from high school walking toward me, her blue eyes sparkling like Mom's. I hadn't seen her in years, but she and a few others from our high school youth group who lived in the area had heard the news and came to be with us on that cold December morning. Friends who knew me in the context of "Mrs. Wright's" daughter. Friends who knew Mom, shared the warmth of her kitchen, and her empathetic ear.

When I came home to Nashville, friends here responded with their own ways of comfort. Two friends had separately left me quiet packages of recovery. They didn't need me to be there to receive them or to sit and converse. A warm bathrobe and video collection of classic movies filled a cheerful gift bag, and a pair of whimsical pajamas and bath oils were neatly tucked into another. The message from both motherless daughters lovingly receiving me into my own pain was, "Take time to be quiet and rest, you will need it." They had been there. They knew.

Other friends brought gifts and called to ask in detail about how the service was, or how I was feeling today. Piles of cards came in, full of comforting voices offering me their company in my pain and reminding me of God's mercy. Emails, just checking on me, peppered my inbox. One friend brought a huge and cheerful poinsettia and three loaves of homemade bread to fill the holiday emptiness. Another friend dropped off lotion and soaps with a handmade card by her young daughter, naive drawings of angels and tender crayoned words of love. A master of sweets informed me of a wonderful new hot chocolate offered by a refreshing new boutique I must venture out to see. Each gift of love given with the empathy of those wading into the sorrow with me lifted my spirits and carried me a little closer to wellness.

It helped so much for people to acknowledge my pain. Simply saying, "I'm so sorry for your loss" or "we're praying for all of you" relieved me of the burden of having to always tell them, saved me from having to pull out the words and carry my sorrow *to* them. Instead, they met me with open arms and *took* some of my burden. While I know it is awkward and uncomfortable, and difficult to know just what to say, it was always better for people to speak of Mom or her death. Otherwise, unknowingly, the silence adds to the loneliness of the hurt.

My community was living Galatians 6:2, bearing my burdens with me. Whether through the quiet of late-night email, or the gatherings over food or in church, or through voice mail or phone conversations, I am grateful to the amazing saints who intentionally shared my load. This tenderness reckoned the strength of the Lord to me.

Above all, my husband has selflessly laid his life down for me this year, patiently waiting, encouraging, leading, weeping. He fills the empty places with his heart, and he urges me to reach for the mercy of Christ, to simply walk when I am too tired to run. And slowly, my strength is coming back. Little bits at a time, I can begin to turn the conversation in someone else's direction, asking about their needs and hurts as I step outside of the dark room of tears I've been living in. And one day I will be of use, offering back the comfort that was given to me, delivering roasted chickens, making the phone calls, and sharing the sorrow.

# 15

# Higher Purpose

*A finite point has no meaning unless it has an
infinite reference point.*

JEAN PAUL SARTRE

*God whispers to us in our pleasures,
speaks in our conscience, but shouts in our pains:
it is His megaphone to rouse a deaf world.*

C.S. LEWIS

❦

The experiences of the last year, everything from the
initial diagnosis to Mom's final days, brought to the
foreground questions that have branded creation
since the defining day in Eden. "Why?" "Is there anything that
can be counted on?" "Is my faith real?" And the one that actually infuses suffering with any meaning at all: "Is there a higher
purpose to what we are going through?"

Philosophers and theologians have attempted answers in
books and treatises. Radical seekers have tattooed existential
answers to eternal questions on arms, backs, and legs. Hucksters
and pitchmen have printed bumper sticker slogans and hosted
TV shows, and in the end, all of the answers have ranged from

good to bad, from practical to ridiculous, from sacred to blasphemous. My own journey has had its fair embrace of some of all of the above. In this season I have actually found comfort in the bottom line awareness that no matter how hard I think, some things will be unknowable until the other side of life. No matter how much I want to know why Mom suffered, and why she died, there are simply things that God has not chosen to allow me to look into now. My desire to eat from the tree of knowledge, to know what I am not intended to know, can send me into a spiraling cycle of frustration and depression, and separate me from the things I can know and be comforted by. My experience has been that answers to some of the questions are variable and malleable, not accommodating to my whims but to the very nature of a dynamic God who is untamable. But the answer to the question of a "higher purpose" to our suffering always comes back to a reflecting of the radiance of His glory.

As I sat in waiting rooms filled with sick and dying people, I begged God for a chance to reveal His glory into the shadows of suffering. I know that Mom and Dad both prayed for that too, and I know that was the meaning that helped them through days they would rather have skipped altogether.

Mom saw each appointment as something more than a clinical checkup, each an opportunity for something greater than her own need and her own suffering. She took the small opportunities gratefully, not demanding a grander stage. She encouraged a tired nurse by telling her how beautiful her blue-flowered scrubs were. A precious doctor bearing the "perfume of Christ" found encouragement as she asked about all the details of his tireless involvement with missions to the Middle East. And I remember the day she called so excited about her opportunity to be more verbal about her faith with the radiation therapist, identifying the lights on the ceiling over her treatment table as being in the shape of the cross. Mom shared with her that there was no better place to be than at the foot of the cross. Then she climbed up onto the table with failing energy, the pain in her back and shoulder making the short time seem so much longer, and submitted herself to that cross every day for three weeks. And God was faithful to never leave her alone there.

My sister beamed with the radiance, ever the servant and grateful for being chosen for the task. On the most bleak of days, she had a beauty that was lit from the interior presence of the Holy Spirit. The strength that rose from both her and my dad were faithful testimony of a God who does not let us go. Every mundane part of Mom's struggle with life was embued with purpose and greater meaning as each of us struggled to find ourselves in a unique position to reflect His glory. It wasn't something that came so easily that it had no cost. Especially for Mom and Dad. It was hard to get up in the mornings after Mom had been throwing up blood through the night, in intense pain from both the cancer and the treatment, her whole body failing her in constantly unfamiliar ways, and Dad trying to sleep quietly beside the wife of his youth, the mother of his children, the one who would not share his twilight years with him. But before stepping into the little white minivan on the way to treatment in downtown Houston, they would ask the Lord to be glorified in them that day.

The times when I was back in Nashville I had difficulty concentrating or applying myself to anything of much significance. I was always near the phone, anticipating the call signaling Mom's decline. But the time needed to be filled, and my anxious hands needed to apply themselves somewhere. I did some mindless sewing and found it to be a perfect project to occupy myself between phone calls to Houston. One of the patterns I used repeatedly inspired me to cut up old sweaters that were in the "retired" pile and use them as the pieces of the skirt. I took turtlenecks, V-necks, and cardigans, and unassembled and reassembled. When the skirt was sewn, the old sweaters were connected in new ways, the sum of their parts producing a greater new whole.

They were undone and reused in ways I never would have imagined. I guess we all were. The curse of this fallen creation is that we will indeed be cut up, unassembled, and torn apart. The higher purpose that gives richness to the poverty of suffering is in surrendering to be reassembled, resewn, and reused as parts of a greater whole, pieces of creation connected in unexpected ways that echo the radiance of His glory.

# 16

# $\mathcal{R}$emembering

*I thank my God upon every remembrance of you…*
PHILIPPIANS 1:3 NKJV

*God gave us memories that we might have roses in December.*
SIR JAMES BARRIE

🌿

I had bought about six books over the last couple of months on the subject of grief. One was a very old little book by a Baptist pastor local to Nashville. I found it in the Belmont University library, and the simplicity of it was so powerful I wanted a copy for myself. So I found a used copy online and ordered it. I also had a book about losing your mother, a book on resiliency, and a strange book with some unusual thoughts on dark emotions. Each of the books were somewhat helpful, though none of them were read cover to cover. Most were a little too clinical for me to trust the sorrow of the authors as honest, but there were bits and pieces I am grateful to have been given. I put them all away in my library in the middle bedroom of our home this week. Most of the bookshelves are full, but I moved and shuffled enough to fit the last of them in.

The closet in that room is filled with bookshelves too. In fact, most spaces in the house that sit empty for very long are soon filled with bookshelves. I am pretty good at clearing out and getting rid of things, so most of what is on the shelves is valuable to us. The shelves in this closet store things important enough that the "throw it out" freak in me is not allowed to touch. The shelves start at waist level and go up to about 18 inches from the nine-foot ceiling. These shelves are filled with memories. Both Jim's and my high school yearbooks sit in the upper dark corner on the top shelf. Next to that are college yearbooks, diplomas, awards, and personal photo albums from childhood. The photos are yellowing, and more fall out of the books each time I pull them down to page through them. The other shelves are home to our wedding albums, various vacations documented in individual albums, career photos, and small gift bags full of unmounted random photos and negatives. I also store books my grandfather made that hold his original hand-painted signs, jewelry designs, and tattoo patterns. Photos of the father my husband never knew sit in a box, and my cap and National Honor Society tassel are underneath a box of sentimental memorabilia. There is a small box that houses poems Mom wrote as a child, with naively drawn illustrations. I pulled them down while my sister was here over the holidays and we dropped fresh tears on the old papers. The closet is a keeper of life's souvenirs, neatly stored.

Lately, my memories of Mom are not so neatly stored. They come in waves running over me all at once, and then there are times when I am dry and find it hard to retrace her face in my mind. I know I have retained memories, and I know there must be a way to enter them, to browse them with joy. Perhaps they just need some organizing.

The other night I was reading a book in bed. From nowhere the vision of Mom's last few minutes came into my mind with the rush of a tornado, ripping up the delicate seedlings of peace that were growing in my heart. The memory wasn't as it actually was though. The memory was a terror, a distortion of the actual gentle moments of her last few breaths. It was an assaulting memory that set me into a tremulous sorrow. My sleeping husband woke up to hold me and reassure me. I knew I would need to capture and intentionally manage my memories for a while.

There have been other assaults. Sad and pitiful pictures of Mom come into my head, and I am overwhelmed by the last few months of her life. I see her shuffling from the house to the car on the way to a doctor's appointment. I remember her hunched over in a wheelchair cupping her head in her hands, cold from fever and aching from too many things. I can see her desperate for water in the hospital, tearing off her oxygen mask to try and sip through a straw, the oxygen saturation numbers dropping furiously. She would struggle to get the mask back on, and we would will the numbers to climb, her asking, "How'm I doing?"

The good part of these memories is that they reminded me of how very sick she was, that she was in such discomfort and pain. That makes me glad she is no longer suffering, and I let go of her a little more. But I can only glance at those kind of memories for now; I can't linger on them and examine them. Those remembrances must be gathered into a box and set aside, carefully, for a season. The tenderness and proximity are too close. I can only glance at them the way you glance at a solar eclipse, aware of it but unable to stare because of the toll it might take. For now, I take my remembrances, wrap them in a soft cloth, and tuck them into a hidden place for safekeeping. They will be there when I am ready to unwrap them.

There are other memories that are more gentle in their approach and less wrenching. They are triggers of sight, sound, smell that send me to a "Mom thought." They are different than the assaulting memories that sit heavy and oppressively. They are the everyday sweetnesses that speak of the presence of Mom. They sometimes come out of nowhere like assaulting memories, but I find I can allow them to linger. I can look straight at them and ponder them, and reencounter their goodness.

I was reading again the other night, and the words "peppermint lozenge" triggered a memory. I had sent a little makeup bag full of peppermint lozenges for Mom to keep near her to help fight nausea and dry mouth. I allowed myself to remember shopping for them and for the special little bag, and I remembered looking for the right box to mail it in. I thought about the phone call when she got the package and was so thrilled with it. I made her smile that day, and I lingered on that. It was a sweet memory.

A dear friend gave Jim and me tickets to see Alison Krauss and Union Station accompanied by the Nashville Chamber Orchestra at the Opry House this week. We were tired and a little unenthusiastic but grateful for the generous diversion. When we sat down four rows from the front, I was lost in the evening. I allowed myself to be taken by the sounds, the extremely beautiful musicality that came from the stage, and it swept over me in waves of healing. Triggers of memories happened all night. The second song was called "I'm Just a Ghost in This House." I allowed myself to picture my dad alone with the memory of Mom in the house, and tears silently fell off my cheeks. Then halfway through the night, the musicians stepped back and Alison and two women stepped up to one microphone and sang a tenderly confident "Blessed Assurance." It was the last hymn we sang with Mom in her hospital room, when she pulled off her oxygen mask to sing out the chorus with us. After I wiped all remaining traces of makeup from my face, the next to the last song was an exquisite rendition of "Funny Valentine" with the orchestra. It was Mom and Dad's song. On one of their anniversaries, we all gathered at the beach to celebrate, and one night we brought a boom box down by the water. They held each other close and danced to "Funny Valentine" in the sand. With that memory playing in my mind, the kind woman beside me retrieved tissues from her pocket to catch the sweet tears of remembrance falling effortlessly from my eyes. It was a full night of triggered memories, the kind that can begin to heal your hurt.

I suppose I have begun to enter a season where I can choose certain memories. Chosen memories are not triggered or brought up by assault, but intentionally brought up for the sheer purpose of remembrance. Certainly, remembering the things that made up the best of Mom are a comfort. Her childlike enthusiasm towards life, her consistent trust in the Father's care and sovereign control, her ability to see the best in people, her nurture of her family. I consciously allow myself to wander in these memories.

But I am even finding strength to choose everyday memories. I pull out recipe cards with directions on how to make things she made so many times, and they are written in her handwriting. I remember the smells in the kitchen when she would make that dish. I see her moving from the refrigerator to the counter, retrieving bowls, mixing spoons, and ingredients. The kitchen was a comfortable place for Mom, and I remember her there easily. I choose the sights and sounds of when she was vital and thriving, and I linger there for a while.

I know it is common to almost deify a loved one who has died, and I know I will tend to remember through a filter. That doesn't worry me. I allow the bigness of her goodness to enlarge the memory, but I am not unaware of Mom's endearing foibles and irritating failings. Her strengths *and* weaknesses help redefine myself, and those aspects are valuable teachers for my life. She would offer them willingly, so I try to carefully remember. But the bravery and faithfulness and courage and richness of her memory is far more lasting and consuming in my mind these days.

I am thankful for generous friends who allow me to remember out loud. At lunch or on the phone they patiently hear my remembering and smile or ask for details. I am particularly grateful to my husband for the memories he shares with me about Mom not only from recent years, but also all the way back to when I was sixteen. He knew Mom before we ever dated, and I think he chose his mother-in-law before he chose me, and that's okay with me. He knows her with me in memory now, as he has known her with me these many years.

I am collecting all of these souvenirs and placing them on shelves in the closet of my heart, to take out and look at and examine as time passes. Some of them are stored on the upper shelves that aren't as easily reached, others are in boxes for safe-keeping, and some sit out on the front shelf available at the slightest remembrance. Some will be damp from tears, and others will be tattered from being taken out and examined so many times, like a favorite poem or photo. My closet holds the fullness of life that is worth the risk of remembering.

# 17

# Keep Showing Up

*He who is faithful in a very little thing is faithful also in much.*

LUKE 16:10

*The drop hollows out the stone not by strength,*
*but by constant falling.*

PLUTARCH

❧

It's hard to believe that I have an art show coming up in just a couple of months. Mom was always so much a part of that world with me. She would ask about what I was painting and how the details were shaping up for the show. Then she and Dad would fly in every time, making me feel so special. My shows were something important to them. She would beam over me at the opening, remarking at my growth and the particulars of each painting. This would be another of the painful "firsts." The first show without her.

Right now, I don't feel like a painter. In fact, I haven't painted since last year, and I'm not sure I will remember how to do it. My emotions have been spent in other directions this year. I wonder what images will come to me at the canvas this season.

Lately, I've been going into my studio for just a few minutes each day. I sit in my chair at my table beside my easel and all my paints. I hold a brush in my hand, scratch a pencil across some pads, and then go back upstairs to return to writing. In a few weeks, I will put away my books and computer and put on my painting clothes. They are a comfortable collection of oversized men's khakis and shirts from the local thrift store. They have old paint smeared across them from the last time I painted. There is a lot of paint especially on the right shoulder and right thigh where I consistently wipe my brushes if they are too paint or water heavy. They are the clothes of a painter, and proof that indeed I once painted. I'll pull my hair back out of my eyes, step into my clothes and painting shoes that slip on with no ties or buckles or zippers, and every day I will go into my studio and sit in front of the canvas. Eventually the painter will show up, and I'll be ready for her.

The other day I was talking with my editor about wanting to write about the importance of a tended spiritual life in the season of grief. I spoke of how hard it has been for me, and how I honestly don't feel like working on my spiritual life right now, and that I'm not sure I know how. He said, "You just have to keep showing up."

I suppose, like the painter in me, I must engage in the things of a healthy spiritual life, and eventually I will find myself in the middle of one. I will need to put on the "clothes" that remind me of who I am as a woman of faith, and gather the other familiar tools of spiritual life maintenance.

Because grief colors outside the lines, nothing is as it was. Mom's illness and death have affected everything, even my spiritual life. I have encountered a new expression of God and my faith this season. God in the context of personal suffering looks different than my untested pictures did. I've doubted and rethought a lot of the things I have taken for truth for many years. I'm feeling more confident, more comfortable, but some days it still feels unfamiliar, as though I'm wearing someone else's slippers. Things I have grandfathered into my own faith from other peoples' have been reexamined for honesty and authenticity. And I am more confident of echoes and rumors than audible voices. My youthful faith needed to believe in audible and transcribable encounters, but the reality is that rumors and echoes are what God has given me. As I keep showing up, the rumors and echoes are stronger, closer, more convincing. But it is a struggle to find my way through to more maturing convictions.

I have returned to some familiar tools for the task. Perhaps like holding the brushes that once moved as if they were in an artist's hand, holding the tools from a healthy time in my spiritual life will begin to prod the latent spiritual pulse in me. It will remind me of who I am.

I have not lost my way, even though my way has changed. I am feeling nearness by proximity rather than nearness by closeness. That position, or status, places me as a woman of faith, but I am just a little tired right now. I am face-to-face with the gift of grace in the place of grief. The gift says I don't have to drum it all up myself. Just show up. I know that if I will be patient, time will find me accepting what is, as it is. Through the tiredness, the hurt, the frustration, and even the anger, the Holy Spirit will woo and restore me.

Engaging my will, trusting the Spirit to do, I reach for the tools of faith. I've used my prayer bench as a location for prayer again, giving some form to the pale expression of faith I feel. I've pulled out my friend Robert's book *Venite* as a guide. I've followed daily readings from Spurgeon and various Bible-in-a-year passages. And I've reencountered Oswald Chambers' *My Utmost for His Highest*. Mom and Dad read it together in the morning for years.

I've gathered in the company of other believers for worship and Bible study at our Village Chapel, even when I feel more like sitting quietly at home. I've reinstated practices that were helpful in other seasons, and begun again to use "aspiratory prayers," short sentences inviting the work of the Spirit in my life throughout the day. "Have Your way. Move me from my stillness, Lord." "Fortify my weak places, that I might see You in full face again." "Be present. Come, Holy Spirit." And as Brother Martin Luther said so many times, face to the ground, "Save me, Lord. I am Yours."

The Scripture pictures this season I am in. "Though the fig tree does not bud and there are no grapes on the vines...yet I will rejoice in the LORD" (Habakkuk 3:17-18). Because I remember a time when the fig tree did bud, and the vines were full of grapes, I keep showing up. Even though my spiritual life feels unproductive right now, I remember when it thrived. I look at notes I've written in the margins of my Bible and read through old prayer journals and random pieces I've written on my computer. I spend time quietly meditating on how faithfully God has carried me through the last year, and the forty-four before that. These are all marks on my spiritual clothes, proof of a productive woman of faith having lived here in my skin.

Even though I don't understand, and I don't know if I remember how to do it, I will keep showing up. One day, perhaps, I will find myself in the middle of a thriving spiritual life again.

# 18

# Something Old, Something New

*Until then they wait patiently in the now, looking to the future,
remembering the past, feeling the present.*

R. LOUIS CARROLL

❧

Dad has been home in Orlando for just over a month now. His time here in Nashville with Jim and me for the previous two months, particularly over the holidays, was extremely helpful, extremely sweet, for each of us. There were moments of sharing, reassuring each other of God's comfort and Mom's certain arrival in heaven. We wept privately behind bedroom doors and publicly in each other's arms. We sat under the glow of Christmas tree lights and were warmed by the fireplace, and we shared morning devotions and daily meals around a plastic table in our dining room. There was a sense of familiar, old routines in the context of new ways. And we began to mend.

Lately, we have been able to start to remember together over the phone, and we have even begun to glance at the possibility of future. We are gently allowing some things to be past, and some to be yet to come. That takes us on a journey of "remember when's" and "maybe sometime's." Each of which are uniquely painful, and yet there is joy too. It's sort of like putting ice on a burn; the experience of the two extremes is uncanny in its sense of pain and healing.

Melani and Dan have been in Orlando visiting with Dad for the past couple of weeks, and they have helped him with some redecorating. They rearranged the furniture in the bedroom, and they bought some new art, bed linens, and lamps. There is a sense of comfort in the newness. Not having to see the bedroom the way it used to be takes some of the sting out of being in the room. Mom's hands have not smoothed this duvet or turned off this lamp after reading at night. Some of the ghosts that are just too hard to live with have been tucked away for now. But there is also a need to hold others close. Dad has put Mom's photo, an enlarged version of the one he carried in his wallet when they were dating, on the wall beside the bed. In this, there is comfort in something old and familiar.

Dad has a collection of miniature cars that have until recently been confined to his study. My cousin Cindy and her husband were also just visiting with him this past week, and she told me on the phone that there seem to be cars appearing a little here, a little there. She confirmed that they look rather nice mingled with Mom's teacup collections. Something old, something new.

I have also needed to tuck some things away. For weeks I have carried my keys, lipstick, credit card, and driver's license in the pocket of my coat. I thought I was just trying to simplify my life by not carrying a purse. The other day I added my cellphone, reading glasses, and sunglasses, and found I just had too many things to stuff into my pocket. I looked at my purse hanging on a hook in my closet. It was the purse I carried over the last year during all the hospital stays and doctor visits, the bag I lived out of. While I was sitting in the closet sobbing, I realized that it carried too many ghosts for me, too many memories, and that was why I wasn't carrying it. It has to be tucked away for now. Some things just hurt too much for no rational reason. But I'm learning that it's okay to set those things away, that it doesn't mean I am setting Mom away.

I have, however, enjoyed having Mom's silver compact to put my lipstick on with. The small round disc opens to reveal two little mirrors. The outside is engraved with her initials, and the surface is smooth and shiny from frequent use. Her fingers had touched it, and I hesitated to shine their smudges away. I gave it to her for Mother's Day several years ago. I remember her being so pleased to pull it out of her purse to use when she refreshed her lipstick. And now I tuck it into the small purse I bought today as a temporary replacement for the one I've set aside, and I will use it to refresh my own lipstick and remember her.

Something old, something new. Memories and new beginnings. In a strange juxtaposition, the two sit together to breed healing. At the intersection of the old and the new sits the now.

Abraham and Sarah were advanced in years as they awaited and anticipated the birth of their firstborn, the promised child. When God's promise was fulfilled and Isaac was born, the ironic combination of something old and something new testified of the faithfulness of God. Perhaps that is what we are experiencing, the faithfulness of God to work in strange and unique ways to provide comfort for us in these days.

I was talking with Dad on the phone the other day, just as I used to with Mom. I would discuss with her the things that were heavy on my heart, and she would give me her wisdom and express her concern. But that old habit had to be set aside and tucked away now. As I was listening to Dad's voice, hearing a side of him I hadn't known before, I realized that something new was happening. I was having a conversation with Dad that I never would have had while Mom was alive. And as much as I would give anything to have her back, to have her on the phone, perhaps this was a glimpse of the faithfulness of God. Dad was comforting and advising me. He was now in the first responder seat where Mom had always sat.

I was getting to know in a new way the man that Mom loved, the man she shared her heart with.

At weddings, times of new beginnings, the tradition is for the bride to wear symbols of something old and something new. Maybe we were there, at the altar of new beginnings, experiencing the faithfulness of God in the sharing of memories and the hope of future, in the comfort of the familiar and the comfort of the new.

# 19

# Living in the Land of the Living

*In the midst of winter I finally learned there
was in me an invincible summer.*

ALBERT CAMUS

Someone I love has died. Someone who gave me life, love, care. This experience marks you with a unique scar that may fade, but it will never go away. As many times as I told her I loved her, it is still one time too few. Her death, her dying, were harder than I expected. But now, this grief. It has brought such unexpected levels of sorrow that ache in such unaccommodating ways. How can I find myself reentering life when grief is so consuming right now?

I feel guilty when I even consider it. How can I go back to living when Mom can't? When Dad is suffering so deeply? When everything has changed so much and so permanently? But I know, even against the pain and internal instincts that say to hibernate indefinitely, that hope and healing are found in returning to the land of the living. And I know with all certainty that Mom would want me to.

Life has been moving around me, but I have been huddled off the path for a while. Finding a way to reenter is like double-dutch jump rope. Ropes are coming at different times from different directions, and I have to move my feet and eyes in coordination with the movement. I have to match pace if I don't want to trip and fall. I've never been extremely coordinated, but I have the scars from skinned knees to prove I tried. Trying to find my way back into the land of the living will demand a certain coordination. I will have to concentrate. I'll have to pay attention if I am to find a healthy routine that matches the pace of life, a different life, since Mom is gone.

Part of what is so difficult is that everything is turned upside down. The loss of stability adds to the stress and exaggerates my need for security. I need a safe routine that signals normalcy, whatever that looks like. At the least, all the socks and underwear are dirty, there is no food in the refrigerator, and I discover it has been almost a year since I've had my hair cut. So I can start collecting my life there.

But I can't expect to pick up life exactly as it was. I know there was a version of my life and everything that went with it *before* Mom's death, and from now until forever there will be everything *after*. It is a dividing line in my life history, a point of demarcation. Though I have no choice but to accept it, I can choose to embrace it with new expectations. I have to revise the expectations that were once reasonable. I'm considering making a covenant of "okay's" with myself as I slowly reengage with life.

It's okay to feel a little lost. My confidence level is lower, and I am, in general, more vulnerable. I don't trust my instincts as readily, and I'm not even sure what I think about some issues. Normally I have an opinion at the ready for most anything. But some of my infrastructure has been shaken by the loss of Mom, and I will have to rebuild a little. Her death has redefined my identity, and it will take time to become comfortable and confident in that.

It's okay to not do everything, and it's even okay to not do everything well. I may have to choose some things over others, letting go of some of the things I used to be able to handle. Right now there is a part of me that is unavailable for doing anything other than mourning and comforting myself. That leaves the rest of me, which is less than what I had to work with before. So I may have clean dishes and underwear, but also dirty floors. I may write, but not be able to paint too right now. If I decide in advance that it is okay, I won't be so disappointed with myself.

It's okay to need other people. I may have to lean harder on the people in my life who have offered themselves. I trust Jim to do some of the grocery shopping, and so we have a delightfully full pantry of candy and brownies. I'm trying to say no to the guilt that says I must do everything as the pastor's wife. It's okay to need help with the tasks of nurturing a young church. It's okay to need the cooks from local restaurants, even though I have a wonderful new kitchen. I'll be cooking in my own kitchen again soon, but it's okay to be too tired right now. It is even okay to need Dad to be able to take care of himself without me interjecting myself in his daily routines. And if I find it too hard to jump-start my functioning self again, if the sorrow doesn't lift, it's okay to need a professional therapist or some form of grief counseling.

It's okay to have boundaries, to have places I can't go right now or things I can't do. I love to go to movies, and usually go every week. But I've had to eliminate many of the choices out there this season because they are simply too melancholy for my emotional state. I can't go to certain movies, and I also find that big gatherings are too enthusiastic for me. I am sensitive to loudness, to being overstimulated. So quiet restaurants, shopping at other than peak hours, and arriving a little later to church protects my heart from overspending what is carefully being rebuilt.

There is so much I can't explain or fix. I feel as though I'm moving in slow motion while the rest of the world is on fastforward. There is a lot I don't feel okay about, but I'm trying to get okay. It's hard to regroup and reenter, but I know there is goodness waiting for me there. Psalm 27:13 says, "I would have despaired unless I had believed that I would see the goodness of the LORD in the land of the living." I am merging with the traffic, matching speed, trying to join in. The rest of that verse says, "Wait for the LORD; be strong and let your heart take courage." Perhaps it is also okay to do it a little at a time. At least one day at a time.

# 20

# ℋankies

*He shall wipe away every tear from their eyes;*
*and there shall no longer be any death;*
*there shall no longer be any mourning, or crying, or pain.*

REVELATION 21:4

wo days before my mother's celebration service, a memorial service of joy and hope, my husband told me that my three dear friends would be flying in from Nashville to be with me. Without my having to ask or to be cognizant and functioning, my "girls" anticipated my needs and quietly set about rearranging the schedules of three busy families. As two husbands were traveling, and the third had unpredictable hours, I don't know how children were covered and airline, hotel, and car reservations happened. They called Jim and just told him they would be here.

The night before the service, our generous family from all corners of the United States sat together in the den of what was Mom and Dad's home. The food continued all night, and the stories of remembrance and humor such as only family can share held us together. Me, my sister, and my mom's sister took kitchen duties, but pretty much everyone took care of themselves. No one expected to be waited on, each barely maintaining their own emotional control and not wanting to burden anyone else with more than their load. I looked around the room, and the faces I had seen since childhood were faithfully present to share our sorrow.

My Aunt Gene, having lost her husband eighteen years before, and now all of her five sisters, was abundantly available to my sister, my father, and me. Even in her own loss, she held us together the way she knew Mom would have. My dad's only brother and his wife stopped their lives to come be with us for a week, never signaling any inconvenience or imposition felt from the offering. My uncle's quietly confident and seasoned faith provided security and strength. My only niece, Mom's only granddaughter, drove all night with her husband and two children to share and weep with us in person. My cousin Cindy listened, asked questions, and bled mascara down her face with me. Cousins well known, and not as well known, sipped tea and nibbled cake until a late hour, their very presence a silent and precious sacrament.

Somewhere in the evening, amid the arrivals of family, came the arrival of my friends. Their presence signaled a new layer of my grief, placing me in the context of my own life, motherless now. I expected I would fall apart in their arms, but strangely I was emboldened by their presence. We were now women together, not young girls. And their presence hailed my own reserves of strength and courage, calling up the woman I needed to be in that moment.

And the cousins, aunts, uncles, sister, and father of my family embraced them seamlessly into the fabric of our grieving home.

Before they all left for the hotel that night, the next morning's schedule was discussed and details of travel were gone over. Quietly, my friends handed me three white linen hankies, one from each of them. They wanted me to know that on the hardest day of my life so far, they would be there to help dry my tears.

Our Father does not leave us alone in our sadness. He always provides hankies. Sometimes He sends family or friends; sometimes angels unaware. Once and many tears ago, He sent His Son. To weep with us and to dry our tears. To purchase for us the assurance and promise of heaven, where there will be no more sorrow, no more tears. No sadness of separation haunts the halls of heaven. Jesus' act on the cross has instead purchased us reconciliation with the Father and the fullness of family, the abundance of togetherness. We will all be together again. Mom will clap her hands together once and say, "Hello there, Kimberli Wright Thomas," and there will indeed be no more tears and no more crying.

# Thirty Days
## of
# Meditations

# 21

# An Invitation

*Finally, brethren, whatever is true, whatever is honorable,*
*whatever is right, whatever is pure, whatever is lovely, whatever is*
*of good repute, if there is any excellence and if anything worthy of*
*praise, let your mind dwell on these things.*

PHILIPPIANS 4:8

cripture reading is not just a splint for the broken
spirit, but the very marrow that mends and restores
the bones. During my time of grieving, I have been
uniquely hungry for the truths and reassurances promised
throughout the Scriptures. I have needed to be reminded of what
to allow my mind to dwell on. And even apart from the clear
principles I need to be reminded of, I find that the simple act of
obedience observed in daily Scripture meditation is its own
reward. The rhythm of daily reading yields communion in its
purest form and restores a familiar and refreshing routine to my
life.

So for these reasons, I have included thirty days of meditations
from the Bible. Some were verses we sought out and memorized
together as a family, others were jotted down in some of the many
sympathy cards we received after Mom's death. We devoured each

reference as the intense nourishment it was, and compiled them all in a file for daily readings. They are a combination of encouragement, exhortation, reminder, and affirmation. Some are specific to the subject of grief, others are general topics that deal with the life of a believer in pursuit of God.

I have wept over assurances that my lament is noticed by heaven. The tender picture of our heavenly Father carefully collecting the tears from our eyes in a bottle gives importance to my own crying. I have been steadied by the affirmations of faith calling me to courage. And I have found rest in the truth that it isn't my job to fuel my spiritual energy, but that as the psalmist says, "My flesh and my heart may fail, but God is the strength of my heart and my portion forever" (Psalm 73:26). Henri Nouwen has said in his brief book on the death of his mother that "in our grieving, we wait, already receiving; hope, already possessing; wonder, already knowing. By the presence of the Spirit." I have felt this most palpably in my times of Scripture meditation.

In the months of Mom's illness, there was a whispered theme of unreality, untruth, to every feeling and experience of the day. As we slowly allowed ourselves to realize the things she would never do with us again, she died in us over and over. In those empty moments that flirted with the nihilism of meaninglessness, Scripture reading would reconnect us. Just as we were fainting from exhaustion, we would read of how He gives strength to the weary and that we would mount up with wings as eagles. And we would be quietly restored yet another time. The room would fill with the assurance of God's revealed hope through the message of Scripture. Through this *lectio divina*, the divine reading of Scripture, we prayed the presence of God and invited His still small voice to comfort and carry us over the waves of our sorrow.

In these many days of mourning, I have found this practice a nonnegotiable aspect to my healing. My reading is not so much Bible study, the kind that digs into the history, theology, and application of a passage as it is the soothing balm of the Scripture applied to my wounded heart. As I sit quietly to read over a short verse or verses, I begin by offering a simple prayer of invitation to the Spirit. Then I slowly linger over the words, allowing the Holy Spirit to impress thoughts or pictures on my mind. The gift is given; I don't need to strive. The goodness is deep, and it is indeed the marrow of mending.

The verses from Philippians 4 that urge me to set my mind on true, honorable, right, pure, and lovely things is a direct invitation to the gifts of Scripture. As I am winding my way through this mourner's path, the Bible will be the tool that speaks words of life to my soul, to give me a hope and a future.

# Day 1

1 THESSALONIANS 4:13-18

*We do not want you to be uninformed, brethren, about those who are asleep, that you may not grieve, as do the rest who have no hope. For if we believe that Jesus died and rose again, even so God will bring with Him those who have fallen asleep in Jesus. For this we say to you by the word of the Lord, that we who are alive, and remain until the coming of the Lord, shall not precede those who have fallen asleep. For the Lord Himself will descend from heaven with a shout, with the voice of the archangel and with the trumpet of God; and the dead in Christ will rise first. Then we who are alive and remain shall be caught up together with them in the clouds to meet the Lord in the air, and thus we shall always be with the Lord. Therefore comfort one another with these words.*

Nothing is as comforting as the promise of heaven right now. I've never wanted to go there more, and it has never been more real to me. Mom has given heaven a face.

I don't know the specifics of heaven, what it will actually be like. But I know that Christ's sacrifice made it a promise, and it comforts me a great deal to know Mom and I will be reunited there. I don't know if we will have bodies, or what form they will take. I believe that because God is personal, and has created us with the dignity of individual personality, our redeemed bodies will in some way be distinguishable. We will recognize each other, know each other in an abundance we have not known before.

I appreciate that this passage recognizes that I will grieve. To deny it or somehow challenge me to not grieve would cheapen the reality of life and the value of each life created in God's image. So we grieve. But we grieve with the hope of heaven, which breathes life into the sorrow. These verses bring us back to the foundation of our faith, that Jesus' sacrifice defeated death. And that becomes the template for the rest of history. Death is not the end, but the doorway to what is "next." I lay my head down to sleep, dwelling on that beautiful and unknown "next."

# Day 2

PSALM 34:18

*The LORD is near to the brokenhearted, and*
*saves those who are crushed in spirit.*

❧

t had only been a couple of days since we had received
Mom's cancer diagnosis. The underlying panic I was
beginning to feel was only surpassed by the sorrowful
ache that threatened to choke out any life in my bones.

That night at the Wednesday night Bible study, Jim had
begun a series on the Psalms. He spoke about how beautiful they
are and how you can find every human emotion in them. He
asked that we go around the room and read the verses out loud
from the chapter he had selected for the evening's study. The
phone rang and I excused myself to go answer it, in case it was
Mom and Dad. It wasn't, and when I came back, the verse that
fell for me to read was Psalm 34:18. Jim couldn't have arranged
or manipulated for that to have been my verse that evening; it
happened by circumstance. But I felt as if God had chosen to
send me a personal note. He was reminding me that He understood the depth of sadness I was beginning to feel.

The honest simplicity of the words cuts past the complicated
answers people try to give you when you are hurting. It acknowl-
edges there will be times when we will be brokenhearted and
crushed in spirit, which gives dignity to our pain by not belit-
tling or denying it. The action words "near" and "saves" are
exactly what I need in this moment. The economy of God's message is efficient and sufficient.

# Day 3

## John 14:27

*Peace I leave with you; My peace I give you; not as the world gives, do I give to you. Let not your heart be troubled, nor let it be fearful.*

❧

Peace. It doesn't look the way I always imagined it. I think maybe I expected peace to mean the end of conflict, the end of things being a drain on my emotions, the cessation of all anxiety. I expected a great and grand blanket to fall from heaven, sealing me off from the difficult things of life.

But peace is not emotional detachment, or denial, or a state of unfeeling. It is the ability to function in the midst of conflict, or pain, or suffering. It is the clarity that helps me make wise decisions under pressure. It is the state of being that allows me to sit in the hospital and watch my mom fade from me without running out of the building screaming. And it is beyond description. I can't always define it, but I know it when I'm there. It is a calm that falls on me from heaven, and it is much like a blanket in how it enfolds me, but it does not seal me off from any pain or experience. It just holds me.

Mom tried to give me peace of mind one afternoon. She held my hand as I stood by her bed, and through her oxygen mask she said, "It will be okay, honey. It will be hard for you at first, but the Lord will take care of you." It was as if she spoke an invocation, her words bookended by quick breaths, inviting the peace of the Lord.

My prayers have been short on vocabulary lately. Before Mom died, they were simply, "Lord, have mercy." Lately, they have been, "Lord, grant us peace." It would seem that the brevity of my prayers has not affected the response from God. He is indeed merciful, and His Spirit coats me with just enough peace. Just enough to make the difference in my being able to function. It will be hard at first, but the Lord will take care of me.

# *Day 4*

*He who keeps Israel will neither slumber nor sleep. The LORD is your keep; the LORD is your shade on your right hand.*

❧

There is nothing like the comprehensiveness of the coverage God provides. The love of God seeks me with undeniable and relentless pursuit. When I am in need or challenged by the difficulty of my situation, He is not caught off guard. There is no sleeping savior who has left his watch. He was not surprised by Mom's illness or my sadness. He has not misplaced anything in His universe, and He is aware of my most intimate needs.

He watches with the eyes of a loving Father and functions with the alertness of a personal guard. The picture of the Lord watching over us reminds me of a mother, lingering in the room as her child sleeps, watching for the evenness of breathing, looking to see if a nightmare will interrupt the child's rest. Just the same, at my slightest stirring, He is present.

As the sun is more intense at midday, hotter and brighter, shade sits intimately close to its object, the outlines sharp and distinguishable. The heat of grief has delineated clearly the small plot of shade that is cast by the presence of the Lord, close and within my reach. It perfectly covers me. He intercepts the heat of sorrow burning its way through my heart.

The Lord is alert. He is on duty, attuned to my breathing, covering me in shade. I can afford to close my eyes, for He will not be gone when I open them. I am learning of His careful care.

# Day 5

MATTHEW 11:28

*Come to Me, all you who are weary and heavy-laden,
and I will give you rest.*

❧

It is as if Christ doesn't even have to ask if I'm weary. He knows I am. I have looked for rest in the comfort of a bed and a savory meal. I have fallen into the arms of friends and family. I've sought refreshment in beauty, through books, art, music, and nature. I've used the familiar tools of candles, hot baths, and aromatic oils. They are all good resources for quality rest, but this rest always fades.

I don't count these resources useless; they are a momentary escape from the mourning that makes me so tired. God uses them to come alongside and help. But the rest that will reach into my soul and pull it out of the dark begins with the invitation of Christ to "come to Me."

It is only in the firm embrace of Christ that life-giving rest is rekindled in my overspent soul. Sustained rest, the kind that allows me to wake in the morning having made the most of my sleep, that blesses the gift of a good meal, that endorses the arms of friends, that infuses life into beauty, is sourced in the resurrected Son of God, who knows what it is like to be weary.

This invitation produces a deep exhale from the innermost parts of my threadbare interior. I exhale the toxic burdens of this life, and when my lungs are empty of distraction, I inhale the oxygen of refreshment, a refreshment of body, soul, and spirit that pours over my dry bones.

# *Day 6*

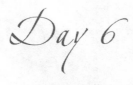

*I will not leave you as orphans; I will come to you.*

Losing my mother has made me a motherless daughter. I feel a bit disconnected from who I am, who I am to be now, without Mom. There are unspoken responsibilities that I take on. I am redefined as a woman, a daughter, and a sister. There is a loneliness that will remain with me until heaven, where we will finally be reunited.

When Christ left the earth, the disciples must have felt an intense loss and lostness. Their whole reason for living had been taken from them. The intimacy of days they had shared in a concentrated three years cut so short. They must have had frightening periods of doubt and uncertainty. I am familiar with these feelings.

One of the most common fears we share as created ones is not "belonging." The lostness that began in Eden still permeates my heart, particularly in these vulnerable times. I long to sense and confirm my belonging to God. In the simplicity of this verse, Christ assures me that I will never be left alone or forgotten.

*So come, Lord. In Mom's leaving, my heart feels orphaned; my belonging is threatened. Would You reassure me with Your long arms, pursue me with Your relentless love?*

# Day 7

*May the God of hope fill you with all joy and peace in believing, that you may abound in hope by the power of the Holy Spirit.*

❧

*I*s it possible that one can never really know the power of the Holy Spirit without having experienced the poverty of suffering? You can't know the strength of a rope until you pull on it.

As I look back over the past months, I see the Holy Spirit giving me hope beyond my own reserves. Any joy, any peace, has been because of the generosity of the Spirit. And at God's initiative. He was "filling" while I was "trusting." This verse tells me that when I am broken-down, reduced to my thinnest veneer of trust, then God slathers on layers of hope without holding back. In the moment I might feel only enough to get through to the next breath. In retrospect, I'm astounded by the abundance.

God is both the source and the object of my hope. Hope in anything other than His ability to give peace or joy will be disappointing to my soul, shallow impressions of peace leaving me hungry for more. Sustaining, substantial peace and joy are found in being a cup that is filled to overflowing. My own efforts can't produce the same. These beautiful attributes of God are in endless supply.

I write these words because I know they are true and not because I always feel them. Grief has often shut down my resiliency and reduced my confidence because of its thievery. So

I feel weak and filled with doubt. But the strength I find is not some evangelical cliché hollow of existential reality. Its truth is based on the reliable track records of ancient men and women of faith, and even on my own more recent experience in the past forty years. I will confess the words of these verses, and allow their reality to be at God's urging.

# Day 8

## ISAIAH 43:1-3

*But now, thus says the LORD, your Creator, O Jacob, and He who formed you, O Israel, "Do not fear, for I have redeemed you; I have called you by name; you are Mine! When you pass through the waters, I will be with you; and through the rivers, they will not overflow you. When you walk through the fire, you will not be scorched, nor will the flame burn you. For I am the LORD your God..."*

❧

In one form or another, this is the most often repeated imperative in the Bible: "Do not fear."

I first memorized this passage when I was nineteen and getting a root canal. It became a prayer when I sat in the dentist's chair, fearful of the entire experience. When I reminded Mom, we smiled at the memory, and we rememorized it together. She said it was a good one to memorize, because of her radiation treatments. "You will not be scorched, nor will the flame burn you..."

God knows me because He formed me, and He knows I am indeed afraid. A lot. Mom's courage came from the One who knew her name, knew her fears. Our very distinct and personal fears are redeemed only in our secure state of "belonging." "You are Mine," He says. It is because of "whose" we are that we are told not to fear.

Even though I know this, my fears still sting, and occasionally they threaten my safe passage. But so far I have not drowned, nor have I been burned. Every time, just when I think I might go under, or suffocate from the heat, a voice reaches through and claims me, and I am again set firm and given that safe passage. It will be so, even today.

# Day 9

## LAMENTATIONS 3:22-23

*The LORD's lovingkindnesses indeed never cease, for His compassions never fail. They are new every morning; great is Thy faithfulness.*

❧

Morning is the hardest time of day for me. Maybe it is because after the dark hours of sleep, the morning sun reveals that things are still as they were, regardless of my dreams. Mom is still gone, the sadness still here. I fall asleep on the greatness of His faithfulness, but I wake to the heaviness of my doubts.

Sometimes I am afraid that I have overtaxed the goodness of the Lord with my relentless neediness. I have put in too many requests for mercy, and surely it will run out at some point. The achiever in me feels I must learn to be more careful, more worthy of His mercies. But I can no more collect them with my efforts than I can catch the rain in my hands as it comes down. It must fall on me, this rain of lovingkindness.

These timeless and classic verses appear out of the midst of Jeremiah's heartfelt lament. He is walking amid the rubble of Jerusalem, lamenting the destruction that surrounds him. And in the midst of that ruin, he records these verses of God's faithfulness. In the broken-down city of his people, Jeremiah still saw the mercies of God.

In the midst of my personal sadness, in the ruins of my grief, there is this promise for daily renewal of the Lord's compassions.

In the midst of all that is changing, God is unchanging. He is reliably constant with His unfailing compassion. John Calvin has said that God hastens to succor those in misery. When so much around me seems unreliable, still God shouts His reliability and wraps it up in daily deliveries to my heart.

This promise says that the compassion of the Lord will be just as relentless as my own neediness. I am simply astounded by this. I beg God to let it sink in, to recapture my mornings with His lovingkindness.

# Day 10

*Those who sow in tears shall reap with joyful shouting.*

❧

*L*ife, like a seed, takes time to grow into something. There is the sowing, the growing, the maintaining, and then the reaping. I have rarely been patient for anything, process being at the top of that list. I say that if there is to be joyful shouting, let's just get on with it. Why must there be this season of sadness and sorrow?

But the Father has set all of life in motion, and it moves at the speed of His urging.

I won't plant perennials that don't flower in their first year. I usually prefer the shallow thrill of a few extra annuals in my garden rather than going through a season without flowers. As I grieve Mom's death, I've wondered why we must experience this separation with those we love, this season without blooms. If heaven is promised us, and if we are not about earning it here in this life, let's just get on with the heavenly joyful shouting.

The sowing in tears is the sweetness that prepares the ground for abundant harvest. My sorrow presses up against the joy I feel a little more of each day, and this contrast intensifies the feeling. Each tear that falls on my fallow and dry heart softens it to again enjoy the intended abundance of this life. There may be a few less flowers this year, but they will be more appreciated next year.

# Day 11

PSALMS 116:15

*Precious in the sight of the LORD is the death of His godly ones.*

⚜

It is strange to think of Mom as more precious to anyone than she was to us. But as difficult as it is for me to believe, as much as I loved her, God loves her more. Her passing was not unnoticed by His gaze, unimportant to eternity. It was uniquely precious by His knowing her name and face.

This verse speaks loudly of the value God has placed on each individual life. Death is not an abstract principle but a travesty of the Fall. Even Jesus wept at the sorrow it extracts.

The Lord having taken notice, having set His gaze on her final appointment, gives significance not only to Mom, but to the pain I feel in losing her. So much emotion is spent and so much of my very life drains from me as I dwell on her passing, but my eyes rest when I read that her death is "precious" in the sight of the Lord.

"Precious" connotes both a mournful sadness and a joyful celebration. What a paradox this grief is. I am so comforted that it is a noticed occurrence, well within the radar of the heavenly Father. Even though He has defeated death, He is aware of the difficulty of its experience for His most "precious" creation. Mom didn't just slip unnoticed out of this life into an unknown fog. Her death was an appointment that God set before time began, and He took personal notice of it, highly esteemed it, and cherished her. He dressed in heaven's finery to escort her from the pages of this life into the grandness of heaven.

# Day 12

PSALM 109:22

*I am afflicted and needy, and my heart is wounded within me.*

☙

*I*nterruptions of wellness, of wholeness, are called wounds. In my sorrow I am hemorrhaging the wellness of my soul. I wonder, *If I apply a compress, will it stop sometime? Can I stop the bleeding long enough for healing to begin?*

Wounds that are deep will eventually heal, but they will likely leave a mark. A mark that says, "I was here, and I survived this intrusion." People say you must give grief time, and that time will heal the wound. Perhaps, but there will indeed be a scar.

I had lunch with a young girl the other day who is bright and sensitive and creatively vibrant. In her blonde dreadlocks she spoke to me of her tattoos and their well-conceived meanings. "Because," as she said, "my body is a text."

Perhaps Mom's death will leave a scar on my heart, a sort of unplanned tattoo. The wound indeed healed, but the mark appearing, the text being written. As time passes and my heart is stronger, I remember Mom with a sweetness that doesn't sting as much. The text reads, "Scarred by pain, transformed by joy."

As I write, it is the second week of the season of Lent, and I am reminded that Christ Himself suffered five distinct wounds that tattooed a text on His body. The text, "Death is swallowed up in victory."

Sacrificial wounds, radiant scars.

# Day 13

## ZEPHANIAH 3:17

*The LORD your God is in your midst, a victorious warrior. He will exult over you with joy, He will be quiet in His love, He will rejoice over you with shouts of joy.*

uring Mom's sickness friends gave us a CD their church had recorded. It was well done, efficient, and tasteful—not overproduced. In its honesty of heart, this offering of worship comforted me in my most restless and anxious moments.

Two songs were my favorites. One spoke of resting in the confidence of God's design, and the other was taken from this passage in Zephaniah. It creates such a picture of promise, and it was in such contrast to Mom's pain and suffering. God is present in the middle of our battles, whether they are physical or emotional, and He is our conquering hero. Yet right after that aggressive image, the Scripture sets a contrast of Him quieting us with His love. In the middle of our worst experiences, when it looks as though all is going down, beyond the veil of our seeing He is very present and protecting us. His rescue is acute, and His pleasure in us results in a celebration of deep joy and honor.

As Mom was fading into the morphine, I would sing quietly down beside her ear, my cheek on her pillow, "He will rejoice o-o-o-ver you...if you could only hear His voice, you would hear the Lord rejoice..." I prayed my voice would somehow meld into the heavenly chorus rejoicing over her, and that at the appropriate time, my small voice would fade softly as heaven's crescendoed.

The day she died, I sang this song to myself, as my own battle with grief became more ferocious. "The Lord our God, is with you, He is mighty to save…" I think perhaps she joins in on the chorus with me now, "He will rejoice o-o-o-ver you…"

# Day 14

PSALM 94:19

*When my anxious thoughts multiply within me,*
*Thy consolations delight my soul.*

❧

There are times when anxiety is so great I want to just go to sleep and wake up next spring, sometime after the rain. The memories are too fast and too full, and I miss Mom too much. I pick up the phone to call Dad, and my cell phone reads, "Mom and Dad." A Post-it Note on my computer lists the things I am praying for, and the top item is "Mom." I reach for a recipe, and it is written in her hand. I am undone by ruthless grief.

There have been times when I have so many anxious thoughts I am overrun by my own sadness. Reading this verse, the promise of it so glaringly simple, is somehow enough even if the consolation were not en route. I am grateful for God's creativity, His relentless pursuit in consoling my soul.

If anxiety threatens to outrun my peace just when I can no longer bear the sadness, God celebrates something in my presence. Something as random as my two schnauzers bursting out to "sing" with Andrea Bocelli on the radio. Howling their little voices in emotional expression beyond any human realm, I am consoled by the delight they bring to my soul.

There is consolation in a silent walk or holding hands with my husband in the morning sun. Consolation in the humor of Dad's dishwasher experience producing eight inches of suds as a result of him filling the dispenser with liquid soap. Our voices filling each other's ears over the long-distance connection, my soul is consoled by his sincere laughter, even in the midst of his mourning. I shared consolation with my sister, sipping a deep porridge-type hot chocolate the night before she and her husband went home. The goodness of taste lingering on my lips after she left. Consolation in the generous souls who surround me and lift me before the Father in my weakness, where I will be quietly restored.

# $\mathcal{D}ay$ 15

*As for me, the nearness of God is my good…*

✿

With all the tools of comfort available, my wellness is always best facilitated by my proximity to God. He desires my highest good. I am surrendered to that principle. I experience the reality of it by His nearness.

Celtic spirituality has a concept that recognizes places, people, and experiences when the distance between us and God is at its smallest. They call these experiences "thin places." It is like when a sunset makes you feel as if you are peeking behind the curtain of heaven, and you sense the eternal right in the midst of the temporal. Or when you spend time with someone and wonder later if perhaps you had unknowingly visited with an angel. The provision of peace, or comfort, or encouragement seems to have had the distinct scent of heaven. The seen and the unseen world are in their closest proximity in these times.

The day Mom died, I was sitting on her screened-in porch at the house. I was bathing in the brightness of the warm filtered sun, remembering the nickname Mom gave her friend Mary, "Mary Sunshine." Mary in turn called Mom "Sparkle Plenty." In that distinct moment, the sun glittered down the waterway some twenty feet from the back porch. I had prayed for God to allow me to sense Mom in some way after she passed, and in that thin place on the screened-in porch, I saw the water "sparkle plenty." The wall between this life and heaven was transparently thin for just that moment, and I felt the nearness of Mom, heaven, and God.

# Day 16

PSALM 119:28

*My soul weeps because of grief;*
*strengthen me according to Thy word.*

❧

The tears of the soul acknowledged in this passage connect me to an ancient fellowship of grievers. More than three thousand years after this was written, I say the same words, cry the same tears. Tears cried in grief melted the soul of the psalmist, and the tears I cry over Mom have done the same to mine.

Charles Spurgeon said tears were liquid prayers. If this is so, I have prayed without ceasing. I have moaned the prayers of sadness and wiped them on my sleeve, dripping a bit of my soul with each tear. My pillow has given ear to these liquid prayers, and the Spirit has given them words, as He intercedes on my behalf before the Father.

This verse from the richness of the Psalms tells me that as I weep, I will be strengthened by His Word. As I meditate on Scripture, and contemplate the truths of my faith, I will be strengthened. It is a phenomenon that once again speaks to the intimate attention God pays to those He calls His beloved. I have not had to drag myself to Scripture out of some hollow ritual. I have been "given" a hunger for Scripture that drove me in willing obedience to the Word. It is just like God, who gifts us with rescue to begin with, to place the desire within me for what will result in my highest good. I find I have had the experience before having known the promise. I have been strengthened by His

Word without having intentionally pursued it for that purpose. His faithfulness "hears" my tears and then gives me a hunger for the Word, which feeds me with the nourishment of His very sacrifice, the bread of life to restore my soul.

# Day 17

ISAIAH 58:11-12

*The LORD will continually guide you, and satisfy your desire in scorched places, and give strength to your bones; and you will be like a watered garden, and like a spring of water whose waters do not fail. And those from among you will rebuild the ancient ruins...*

❧

In this passage we discover a comprehensive prescription of wellness. The poetic form is so inviting, and the pictures are directly relevant to the emotions of a griever. I am in need of what this verse promises.

I have a sense of lostness from being in the valley of the shadow of death, and I need guidance to find my way. In the long pause of grief I have stepped out of my life, and the path back to it is found in one guided and revealed step at a time.

I need to be satisfied, not with fading confections of temporary satisfaction, but with what will be God's highest good for me. If there has ever been a time when surrender to that was more appropriate, I haven't encountered it.

My weary physical state produces fragile bones needing to be fortified. My immune system is worn down from the lack of rest and good nourishment, and I am vulnerable to illness. Typically, just after I have gone through a stressful time, I have a bout with bronchitis, or a sinus infection, or the flu. This time I have remained remarkably healthy. It is attributable only to this promise.

The dryness of my spirit is addressed, and Isaiah says that God will meet my needs in that area too...in abundance.

My wellness is further prescribed. The ruins of my despair must be rebuilt. In Patricia St. John's poem *The Alchemist*, she says that God will rebuild "cementing sad experience with grace" and fashion a stronger temple. Isaiah says God will indeed restore and rebuild what was razed in sadness. Only three chapters later he promises the mourner "beauty for ashes." I wait in anticipation for this goodness.

# Day 18

PSALM 56:8

*Thou hast taken account of my wanderings; put my tears in Thy bottle; are they not in Thy book?*

≈

The "lostness" of grieving is uniquely draining. Mom, the familiar tether that has discreetly anchored my life, is gone and I am adrift. Fortunately, my lostness, sending me into a windless, silent, wandering, has not gone unnoticed by God.

It would seem that He has been attentive to my mourning. I have thought I was alone at times, confusing silence with isolation. But He has been ever close, close enough to catch my tears in a bottle as they fall from my eyes. What science calls "lacrimal waste," God has valued, counted, noted, and saved. He has been near enough to make a record of each unique drop. This Scripture speaks eloquently of His presence, reminding me of my state of belonging.

What kind of loving God is attentive to this detail of my life? How can I not be comforted by His intimate amassing of the remnants of my sorrow? I wonder if perhaps the bottle of my tears might sit on the shelf next to the tears Jesus wept. A Savior acquainted with my grief, who wept at the grave of Lazarus His friend, most likely weeps at the death of each of His beloved ones, weeping for each by name. Including "Ann," my mom.

The closeness of God, who takes notice of my sadness, and the empathy of the Son, who weeps with me, is another reason I am more than humbled at being a "daughter" of God's family. This family of faith enfolds me: shamelessly sorrowful, woefully inadequate, and yet unquestionably kept track of, recorded in His book.

# Day 19

## PSALM 31:10,14-15

*For my life is spent with sorrow, and my years with sighing...But as for me, I trust in Thee, O LORD, I say, "Thou art my God. My times are in Thy hand."*

This is an example of a psalm of lament. Much of the Bible, in fact, is lamentation. The books of Job, Lamentations, Jeremiah, and Habakkuk are largely laments. In my season of grief, it is a comfort to know that Scripture gives us a model for engaging in authentic and faithful lament.

The psalmist poured out his sorrow and hurt in honesty to the Lord. I find I am too tired sometimes to know the words to express my hurt, my anger, my uncertainty. The written laments of Scripture can facilitate my own speechless sorrow. They also allow me permission to be frail in my humanity and express it honestly to God. There are those who would rush the mourner to joy without allowing for the purging of sorrow and anger. I am grateful for the inclusion of lament in the Bible. It causes me to be more trusting of a God who allows me to express the rawness of sorrow, even when tucked inside the delivery of rage.

Matthew Henry said, "The faithful lament their calamities and hope in God's mercies." The psalmist lays out both expressions in Psalm 31. In the affliction of my sorrows I lament, but it is only by God's mercy and my placing my hope in Him that I am rescued. Hope keeps the lamenter in me from falling into despair. A healthy lament is always grandfathered in by hope in the mercies of God.

# Day 20

*Moreover, I will give you a new heart and put a new spirit within you; and I will remove the heart of stone from your flesh and give you a heart of flesh.*

There was a time in my grieving when I honestly was afraid I would never feel again. It was so odd and unfamiliar. Because in my more typical state, I am emotional Velcro. Emotions stick to me. But for almost two months after Mom's death, I was stone.

At first, I thought, *Well, I'm handling this better than I thought I would.* It was indeed a safe place to be, behind a heart of stone. I suppose that when you experience such deep sorrow, your heart puts up a support wall, a defensive measure designed to protect the interior places from further damage. I guess that I just shut down certain parts of me in order to put all my energies towards trying to function in the midst of loss.

But when the time came, I "felt" as the Father would gently remove the stones, a bit at a time. I would ache when I remembered. I would cry instead of weep. I would be moved by someone reaching out to comfort me or Dad. I could absorb gestures of love from strangers whom we would have to tell our story to, the stone melting a little more with each touch of heaven wrapped in humanity.

The heart of flesh that is mine again is welcome. The protective season of stone served me, but the heart of flesh is what God intended for us to carry. It senses His presence more readily, and responds to pain or beauty, love or loss. It is a risk to use it, but it is also a gift.

# Day 21

## REVELATION 21:4

*He will wipe away every tear from their eyes; and there will no longer be any death; there will no longer be any mourning, or crying, or pain; the first things have passed away.*

🌿

There is a new world, the "not yet but yet to come," when there will be no more sorrow, no more separation. None of the soul-breaking feelings I have carried these last months. It gives ease to my ache to know that on the other side of the curtain, Mom is finished with her crying, her tears, her mourning. In completeness she waits for our reuniting, free of pain at last.

Typically, the concept of heaven is so abstract as to be almost frightening. The unknown experience is a risk to our sensibilities. I wonder if, when in the womb, someone were to tell us about another place, a place of unimaginable experiences and beautiful light, if the unknown nature of it would cause us to reject the invitation? If given the choice, would we ever have chosen to go to that place intentionally? Would we choose birth over the familiarity of the warm and cozy womb?

Perhaps that is like the passage from this life to heaven. Because of the mystery, we are afraid to leave the familiar "womb" of this life for the unknown wonders of eternity.

I am glad God chose to send comfort in His written Word, whispered details on this "yet to come." The written revelation records the description of a most desirable destination. It is a truth made sure, a reality I will share with Mom, her "already," my "yet to come." It is paradise regained, the tree of life once again in full fruit. Life as it was always intended to be.

# Day 22

*For I am convinced that neither death, nor life, nor angels,*
*nor principalities, nor things present, nor things to come,*
*nor powers, nor height, nor depth, nor any other created thing,*
*shall be able to separate us from the love of God, which*
*is in Christ Jesus our Lord.*

❧

What do I cling to when I am most afraid? What can I count on to stay constant? Where do I fill my soul when sorrow is draining it of hope? What is my definition of security? These are the defining questions of my season of grief.

I am coming to understand that I cannot cling to the corruptible creation, the mortal expression that God has so eloquently packaged in flesh and blood. I cannot put my security in my life or the lives of those I so deeply love. I can't count on any of the created universe to safely sustain my hope.

At the core of my sadness over Mom is the separation of death. And at the heart of that sadness is the quiet doubt, rubbing against my faith, hinting that if I am experiencing this separation from Mom, then perhaps I can even be separated from God. Death is the single experience that hints of our own separation from God, the ultimate result of the Fall. It is the grief I experience that helps inform me of my acute need for the rescue of Christ.

Whether the Holy Spirit inspired Paul's declaration in these verses through existential conviction wrought in the crucible of experience, or theological deduction proved by thoughtful consideration of the subject, it bursts from Scripture with poetic elegance and comprehensive confidence. And it infers the questions behind questions like mine. Paul's affirmation posits that nothing in the entire vocabulary of creation, no condition of heart or proximity of body, can impair the comprehensive reach of God's invincible love.

This is the answer to my questions, the answer that claims my heart with the stubbornness of conviction.

# *Day 23*

ECCLESIASTES 3:4

*A time to weep, and a time to laugh; a time to mourn,*
*and a time to dance.*

*I* am sometimes impatient with the continuing season of my grief. And I feel the imagined pressure of others looking on, urging me to be done with it, to move on. You can always tell the ones who have not been here, who have not walked the mourner's path. Their intentions are good, but their delivery is short of the generosity proved by firsthand empathy. Their comforts come in clichés and safe statements that don't invite detailed responses that might engage them in your grief. They are more stingy with the time to weep, more urging of a time to laugh.

When you have been there, marked your own days on the walls in the cavern of weeping, you wear your empathy up front, careful to offer nurture to the fainting soul before you. I didn't know, before now, before I had been here.

This verse, isolated from the rhythmic list of "a time for's," proclaims a sweet languorishness to the pace of these seasons. It stretches out with the plenty of abundant patience. There is no hurry to the lyric, no urgency to the measure.

Koheleth, the voice of Ecclesiastes, sets the poetic couplets in the rhythm of breathing. Breathing out the setbacks and sufferings of life, we next breathe in the merciful delights of creation.

I hope that as I exhale the sufferings and inhale the mercies, I will become acquainted with a new, more propitious cadence to my days. An unhurried tempo that makes time for desperate petition and remembers to express grateful praises, that draws on the strength found in perfect submission to the speed of God's unhurried intentions.

# Day 24

GALATIANS 3:3

*Are you so foolish? Having begun by the Spirit,*
*are you now being perfected by the flesh?*

❧

Even the experience of my mourning is colored by my inability to completely grasp the reality of grace.

I grew up, gratefully, under the direction of vital faith that was evidenced by our family attending regular church services. I earned my share of attendance pins and verse memorization ribbons. And from an early age I'm afraid I assimilated a performance-oriented faith toxic to true worship and discipleship. At no fault of those who loved me, I fell in line with an unspoken tutelage in American evangelicalism that urged me to earn and work for God's approval.

I would never say it, but I was probably quietly convinced that there was a strong possibility I did not send Christ to Calvary because I was actually such an efficient, low-sinning Christian. I didn't do so many bad things and did do so many good things. The better I did my Christian walk, the more my heavenly Father loved me.

I have since, in my adult years, come to wrestle with the ever-so-important concept of graceful faith. Grace is God's most generous extension of His love to me, assuring me I am secure by His having chosen me, not my having caught His attention with my elaborate efforts at spiritual success.

And now at my mother's death, I worry that I will "do" grief wrong, somehow disappoint God in my lack of resiliency or with my faintness of heart. I am afraid my coming up short somehow proves me the faker I truly am. But as my interiors are laid open and unprotected before the mercy of God, as I relinquish the controls of my spiritual success, I find that anything other than surrender to the grace that chose me as I am would be blasphemous, trying to complete in my flesh what was begun for me, and in me, by the Spirit.

# Day 25

## PSALMS 130:5-6

*I wait for the LORD, my soul does wait, and in His word do I hope.
My soul waits for the LORD more than the watchmen for the
morning; indeed, more than the watchmen for the morning.*

❦

*I* have never been good at waiting. I want to see around the corner *now*. This year has not been much different. We have waited for doctors, waited for test results, waited for drugs to take effect, waited for bodies to mend. We have waited for airplanes, waited for phone calls, and eventually waited for death. My patience has been tried and usually found wanting.

I have tried to wait with patience and to wait expectantly. There were little gains along the way, times when Mom's test results came back good or when a new medication eventually gave her relief. Some of the doctors were kind and caring, worth waiting for. Some waiting rooms were sanctuaries away from busyness. But usually, whatever I set my sights on eventually gave way to disappointment.

There is a deep sense of longing presented in these verses from Psalm 130. My soul waiting, and then my soul waiting even more than the watchmen wait for morning. Morning is certain, a law of nature, and the night watchmen have it as the object of their waiting. But even as certain as morning coming, my soul waits *more* certain of the Lord meeting me in my place of need. That is an expectant waiting, one that does not end in disappointment.

I believe that even in the moments of waiting for good news about Mom's health, even when her body ultimately failed and my waiting was greatly disappointed by that result, my greater hope in the Lord was not disappointed, and He met me in the context of my pain.

This greater hope can transform my waiting in specific areas, giving it a greater context, greater than the details of circumstance. But ultimately any waiting, any longing, will only be satisfied in heaven, in the eternal presence of God. That is the ultimate object of my waiting, and I wait eagerly with the psalmist, more sure of it than I am of morning. Maranatha. Come, Lord Jesus, come.

# Day 26

*We also exult in our tribulations, knowing that tribulation brings
about perseverance; and perseverance, proven character; and
proven character, hope; and hope does not disappoint, because the
love of God has been poured out within our hearts through the
Holy Spirit who was given to us.*

---

For a steel blade to be rendered exceptionally hard,
it is heated, hammered, and tempered. It must be
heated to its critical temperature, the temperature
at which certain changes in the chemical composition take place,
and then cooled quickly so that it doesn't revert to its original
composition. The exactness in the heating and cooling process,
combined with the hammering and compressing, will result in
steel that is hard. Not brittle like glass or soft like copper, but
tough. If an edge is determined not to be strong enough, the process is repeated.

Evidently, the laws of nature, and the apostle Paul, imply that
struggle makes things stronger. I have known this principle for
most of my life. I have not always welcomed its inevitability or
made myself readily available to the refiner's fire or the forger's
hammer. It is perhaps an axiom best appreciated in retrospect,
less in anticipation.

In the middle of this past year, when the confirmation of
Mom's diagnosis was irrefutable and we were aware of her pre-
carious condition, beads of sweat broke out on my soul as I felt

147

the temperature rising. I begged God not to use the hammer, begged Him to consider skipping this season. It is a mysteriously tender horror, this tribulation stuff, gently cuffed by the love of God and the presence of the Spirit. The painful struggle begins, and I am in it before I know, perseverance being subtly wrought in my life. Bad news slowly becomes less debilitating, hope more ready and stabilizing, and then the process repeats.

Until one day I wake up and find I feel a little better, even hopeful. Stronger, tougher.

# Day 27

2 CORINTHIANS 10:5

*We are destroying speculations and every lofty thing raised up against the knowledge of God, and we are taking every thought captive to the obedience of Christ.*

❧

houghts are the most vulnerable part of my daily existence. In the private silence of my imagination, anxieties collect and my rest in Christ is threatened. Every untamed thought in opposition to trust frustrates the path of disciplined belief for me.

The outward struggles of the body, things like eating and laziness and self-destructive behavior, I find more easily controlled. But my mind can quickly sabotage the tender beginnings of goodness. With lethal efficiency I imagine possible conversations and potential situations, and speculate myself into a corner of anxiety. This is completely in opposition to a mind stayed on Christ, to thoughts captured by His desires for my highest good.

I don't know why my tendency is towards worry and "what-if," why I don't simply rest more in the knowledge that God is holding the universe intact. But I find I just begin to make peace with Mom's death, and then I am imagining who will be next, what new sorrow will approach me. God has barely just given me manna for today, and I am worrying about it spoiling and if there will be any tomorrow and will it be good? My thoughts must be persuaded and my disposition set towards obedience to Christ. In the fertile delta of my well-watered imagination, I have asked the Spirit to plant the seeds of transformed thinking.

This will call for the art of spiritual self-discipline, the formation of habits that retool my thoughts and imagination, recapturing and renewing the gift of thought. I may have to carefully choose what I feed my mind, choosing to read promises of hope, Scriptures of assurance, and rejecting certain movies, books, or news of despair or contagious melancholy. There is a rule, a way, a habit of thought that willingly dwells on the best possible good, searching out the lovely and the excellent things of God. I want to be captured by those thoughts.

## Day 28

MARK 6:31-32

*He said to them, "Come away by yourselves to a lonely place and rest a while." (For there were many people coming and going, and they did not even have time to eat.) And they went away in the boat to a lonely place by themselves.*

※

What compassion and tenderness Christ expresses to His disciples in these verses. They had just received the news of John the Baptist's beheading. Their friend was gone, and they had been so busy they hadn't had time to eat, much less to begin to mourn. Jesus knew they needed privacy for reflection, rest for their bodies and souls.

The business of grief is exhausting, and rest is often the first thing to go. When we were together after Mom died—my sister and her husband, Jim and I, and Dad—it seemed hard to allow ourselves to rest, to sit still, to be quiet. It was easier to keep moving and be busy with the details of loss. And there were a lot of details to keep up with. There were plans to make for the funeral, arrangements for the memorial service, people to be called, food to be prepared. And then there were closets to be emptied, and drawers to be gone through, paperwork to take care of. There was a life to close.

At first all of this doing was good. The arrangements had to be made, and it gave our bodies time to distract our minds from the reality that would sink in slowly. As the day's details would wind down, and night would fall, depression would slink in and settle like fog on our wounded little family. Dark and quiet rooms did not seem to be the makings for rest.

But rest is exactly what our bodies needed. Especially Dad, who rarely got more than a couple hours of sleep each night. God designed us to respond to a built-in rhythm of work and rest, declaring the seventh day of creation Sabbath, a time for rest and refreshment. In this exhausting time of loss, this same voice invites us to rest. He knows our need for quiet and solitude. In our evenings of sleep, or afternoons of napping, the Father will mend and repair, refresh and restore our tired and worn-out souls.

# Day 29

ISAIAH 61:3

*To grant those who mourn in Zion, giving them a garland instead of
ashes, the oil of gladness instead of mourning, the mantle of praise
instead of a spirit of fainting. So they will be called oaks of righteous-
ness, the planting of the LORD, that He may be glorified.*

☙

This is the essence of the entire story of redemption,
from beginning to end. Restoration, beauty from
ashes, life from death, radiance from scars.

Grieving does not lend itself to beauty. It is difficult to see
the potential good that can come from such devastating loss.
Grieving is messy work. Sorrow is not neat, and no matter how
it is packaged in books, movies, or cards, the fact is that the initial encounter with grief is ugly. It lingers heavy in my nostrils,
the antiseptic smell of hospital rooms and pharmaceuticals. The
atrophied flesh of my tender mother's body hung on her bones
like moss from a tree. The life had indeed left her, the beauty
stolen with death's intrusion.

But that is the view from here, the sights of a fallen creation
in need of redemption.

Our Father has promised total restoration and complete
beauty. Gladness will be given in exhange for my mourning. Fullness for frailty. For my grief to be made beautiful, it must submit
to the redemption that the entire creation cries for. The ugliness
of death succumbs to the beauty of the love of God. He chose to
enter time to make a way for ashes to become beauty. Christ's

153

sacrifice on the cross was the beautiful ugliness that rescues us from the earth.

When our bodies lose the luster of this life, they fade to ashes. But God has rescued our souls out of the dust to remake us in the fullness of His original plan for His beloved. Mom left the fading body she had no more use for to gain her heavenly beauty. My mourning will become gladness in the fullness of time.

## PROVERBS 31:28-31

*Her children rise up and bless her; her husband also, and he praises her, saying: "Many daughters have done nobly, but you excel them all." Charm is deceitful and beauty is vain, but a woman who fears the LORD, she shall be praised. Give her the product of her hands, and let her works praise her in the gates.*

❦

We rise up and bless her, indeed. Mom, your family praises your beautiful life, and we are grateful for the wonder that was you, and the selfless love that came from your hands.

My earliest memories are of holding hands with her. Her long fingers and soft palms would gather my fleshy little hands in hers, and squeeze twice, our silent signal for "I love you." We held hands for years, until I felt too old to hold hands with "Mom" and was ready to trade up for a boy's hand.

Her hands applauded my accomplishments, and more often my failed attempts. Ball games, performances, art show openings, and family gatherings were all christened by her enthusiastic single clap and then clenched fists, indicating her barely-under-control enthusiasm. They turned the pages of her well-worn Bible and pointed me to Jesus. They smoothed the hair out of my eyes, and were dampened by her saliva to clean dirt from my face. They prepared meals for me, felt my head for fever, and flew up in front of me in the car to hold me safe before seat belts were used. Her hands patted everything she folded three times, and sealed love into towels and sheets and clothes.

When I got married, her hands packed up the remembrances of my youth, and they added a plate at the table for a son-in-law she loved and respected and welcomed.

I held her hands the last week of her life, the grateful child under her touch. I stroked skin made paper-thin by high doses of prednisone, the beauty and architecture of her youth still present in the lengthy fingers and tendon-rich backs of her hands. I squeezed twice, and waited for any hint of a return squeeze when she was starting to leave us, and when there was nothing, I trusted that Someone else would take her hand, and I let go, memorizing the feel of her touch one last time, certain of her love for me.

The works of your hands bring great honor to your memory, Mom. And from the ashes of this earth I know God has made you new hands that you raise in praise of the beauty of His holiness, clapping once in barely-under-control enthusiasm at the completeness of your joy.

If you wish to contact the author,
you may do so at:
kimthomasart@comcast.net